♡♡♡

SHARING
the
LIGHT

♡♡♡

Blessings,
G. Shakti-Hill

What the Experts are Saying about G. Shakti-Hill:

"Shakti, the interview we experienced together brought those powerful memories of the past of being women who want to change the planet into a better place. I am honored that we spoke on such a high level together. I look forward to spending quality time with you in the near future."

Delmary, Artist

"In order to share the wisdom, you must first have the experiences. To share the Light you must know you are the Light. Georgia Shakti-Hill is qualified to do both. Read *Sharing the Light* and find out why."

Wally Amos, Motivational Speaker

"Georgia Shakti-Hill is amazing. She has a way that is both simple and profound, a way that immediately lets her guests know that they are in safe hands so that they can be free to go right to the heart of what they wish to share. She is a master. She guides her guests without ever intruding in a way that bring out the truth of them. In a day when there is nothing more important than that we all communicate the truth of our being and learn to think all-inclusively, Georgia's own personal openness calls forth the unique qualities of her guests and blends them into the whole."

Walter Starcke, Author

♡♡♡

SHARING
the
LIGHT

A Guide to Living in Balance in Mind Body Spirit

Georgia Shakti-Hill

**Shakti-Hill House
Publishing**

Published and distributed in the United States by:
Shakti-Hill House, P.O. Box 2715, Fort Myers Beach, FL 33932-2715
(941) 463-8088

Edited by: Pearl L. Mougios, Judy Borden, Micki Walsh and Linda Townsend

Cover Designed by: Edward L. Hill

The author of this book does not dispense medical advice nor prescribe the
use of any technique as a form of treatment for physical or medical problems
without the advice of a physician, either directly or indirectly. The intent of
the author is only to offer information of a general nature to help you in your
journey for emotional well-being and good health. In the event you use any of
the information in this book for yourself, which is your constitutional right,
the author and the publisher assume no responsibility for your actions.

Library of Congress Catalog Card Number: 98-96807

ISBN 1-893379-49-3

10 9 8 7 6 5 4 3 2 1
First Printing, November 1998

Printed in the United States of America

♡ Contents ♡

♡ **Introduction** ♡

Welcome. I'm Georgia Shakti-Hill and I would like to invite you to join me on a Journey. I have been hosting a television program for seven years. We call it "Living in Balance on Shakti-Hill." My purpose has always been to awaken, educate, enlighten and entertain our audiences. Seeking the Universal Truths, honoring all Paths and finding the Love in each message--these are my guidelines. That is my purpose for this book, too. I am writing this book for you. I know that you can experience bliss, peace, health and abundance. That is the natural state of being. When you are not experiencing bliss, peace, health and abundance; you are out of balance. I want to remind you of all the things that you already know . . . how you may live in balance in mind, body and Spirit. It is my belief that you already know everything required to create a beautiful life. Sometimes a review assists us. These chapters are designed to remind you of that perfect state of bliss and how to get there from wherever your Path has taken you.

I will share with you my personal quest and the

wisdom and the Light from my many interviews with authors and doctors and healers and dancers and swamis and monks and visionaries. I have interviewed hundreds of teachers who have a passion to share their knowledge and their gifts. It is the *passion* that is the key. They often use that exact word, passion. They are compelled to sing their songs, paint their angels, mold their clay. They are driven to teach and write of their experiences. The messages again remind us of our Divinity and bump us back on the Path. Truth resonates. That is how it can be measured. Does it ring true? Do you smile and think, "Oh, yes?" Can you say, "I remember?" Are you quietly tearful?

I have enlisted a little help from my *Friends*. Some are referred to as the seekers, the messengers, the light workers, the rainbow teachers, the children of the light and the emissaries of light. Some are called modern mystics. They have come from all over the planet--Russia, New Zealand, England, the Americas. They are the people preparing for the new millennium. They have been prophesied. When they have found their gifts to share and realized their purposes, they come into our Light. You will meet them throughout the book. They have shared their wisdom and their Light in these chapters and on my television program.

We plan to keep these reminders simple. It might suffice to say for the <u>mind</u>, keep a positive mental attitude . . . for the <u>body</u>, eat good quality food and exercise . . . for the <u>Spirit</u>, become aware of your Journey on the Path. We will *Release the Past, Create the Future* and *Surrender to Success.* We will assist you to *Heal the Body, Move the Body* and *Create Your Space.* We will help you to *Find Your Teachers, Meet the Masters* and *Fulfill Your Dharma.*

It is said that the paradigm is shifting. The world is ready and the Universe supports the change. And, the change begins with each of us. We are all connected. We are One. As you make that shift in consciousness, you raise the vibration of all of us. Oh yes, "the changes are comin' on." I am proud to play my role and count myself among those who are willing to usher in this new Spiritual Renaissance. How could we better do that, than through the medium of television? So, I invite you to join me on this Journey. Our sojourn will be a reminder of how to live in balance in mind, body and Spirit. It can take you back to bliss, peace, health and abundance. Blessings to you.

Love and Light,

Georgia Shakti-Hill

Section I "Mind"

♡ Chapter 1 ♡

Release the Past

I began my personal journey to enlightenment in Newport Beach, California, at the corner of the Pacific Ocean and 15th Street. The year was 1983. Of course, I actually had begun this journey on the day I was born. It was in the Fall of 1983 that I became *acutely aware* of my quest. I had survived serious surgery, ended a relationship and opened to a new way of being. This was a powerful turning point in my life. I was in transition and had been awakened to the Path. I had chosen to live in a darling little apartment on the boardwalk of this wonderful Pacific beach community. Books surrounded me. I was reading eight at one time. My mentors and teachers were appearing, as if on cue.

In the past I had taught "positive thinking" and "time management" and "goal setting." Now, a whole new element had been added--spirituality. As a child, I had been trained in religion and taken my catechism. I had perfect attendance pins from church. Mama was a Sunday school teacher. Religion was part of the curriculum at my university. They called it Western Cultural Traditions. Each of the world religions was addressed and each given equal importance, much to my Christian dismay. However, now I was reading about my Soul. My mind wanted to know everything. I was inhaling information and material. When I wasn't reading, I would walk and dance and play along the beach at sunrise and sunset. I jumped into this project with all of my energy and enthusiasm. Each day brought more knowledge and more techniques to hurl me along the Path. One opportunity after another presented itself and I accepted each and every one. I was enthralled with the adventure. I couldn't wait to release the past. The future was so compelling.

Forgiveness is the Key

Gerald Jampolsky's book, *Love is Letting Go of Fear*, was one of those books I was reading and reflecting upon as I sat on the beach in southern California. This book emphasizes the forgiveness principle. Jerry is one of my heroes. He has founded a whole organization dedicated to the philosophy called Attitudinal Healing. That book guided me to *A Course in Miracles*. *ACIM*, as it is succinctly referred to, would become one of the most life-changing elements in my new adventure. At the recent International Conference on Attitudinal Healing I had the privilege of interviewing Jerry, his wife Diane, his son Lee and several of the guest lecturers for my television program, "Living in Balance on Shakti-Hill.". Luckily, for all of us, his message remains the same: **Love is the answer.**

Aeeshah and Kokoman

Among the speakers at Jerry's conference were Aeeshah Ababio Clottey and her husband Kokoman Clottey of the Attitudinal Healing Connection in Oakland, California. They have just finished their book on healing racism and used the principle of forgiveness to move through their past pains. They've created a space for other people to do the same. As young blacks in America, both had been terribly treated and both had to forgive. Aeeshah had joined the Black Muslims in college in order to vent her anger. Kokoman was born in Ghana, West Africa, and had been dismayed at his mistreatment at the hands of his classmates when he came to school in Los Angeles. Aeeshah and Kokoman met through their work in *A Course in Miracles*. They fell in love, married at an Attitudinal Healing Conference and have created the Healing Racism Project and book. Now their purpose is to share love instead of fear. To accomplish that end, they had to confront and release the deep pain of their pasts. Forgiveness has been a key factor in their happiness. Theirs is a success story and a true love story! They are examples of two of our guests with wisdom to share with our audience.

Words of Wisdom:

"Forgiveness is the key to happiness."

--A Course in Miracles

That is one of my favorite lessons from the *ACIM Workbook*. It is a rule to live by that will serve you well. Whom must you forgive? Everybody. Who is the one most important person on the planet that deserves your forgiveness? *You*, yes, *you.* You must forgive **yourself** first and then move onto all others. When do you begin to forgive? Now!

Never Negate Your Past

It was at that time in the Fall of 1983 I began to understand the power of forgiveness. The Universe had set in motion profound experiences that would prepare me to take giant leaps on my Spiritual Path. The pace had quickened. I had no responsibilities to other people for the first time in my life. Reading, meditating and reflecting were my activities. Each day began with a walk on the beach at dawn and ended with a walk at sunset, then back to my books. I was motivated to clear all negativity from my past. The goal was to release it and move on. My purpose was to reach a middle ground of *Nirvana* and allow all of the people from my past to be released, too. Forgiving them was the key. Negating my past was not an option. I had done the best that I could do under the existing circumstances. So, had *they*, whomever they were. Personal transformation was my focus. Everything I read told me to heal my past.

Healing Past Relationships

It is required that you clear each of your past relationships. After healing your relationship with yourself you move on to your parents. You must forgive Mom. She was doing her best. Psychologists tell us that you cannot form healthy relationships with women until you clear your mother issues. You cannot have healthy relationships with men, if you have not cleared and healed your father issues. It is then easier and faster to move through the *Forgiveness Process*. Forgive all other people from your past: old boyfriends, husbands, wives, siblings, bosses, the list goes on and on . Forgive them all. That lightens your load. It allows you to be free. It creates the space for you to love and trust others. That is powerful!

Words of Wisdom:

"Never negate your past. You did the best that you could do under the existing circumstances."

Louise Hay and Forgiveness

Louise Hay serves as the perfect example of forgiveness and success. Her writings and workshops have healed millions of lives. She graciously agreed to meet me in La Jolla, California, for an interview. When we chatted about her book, *Empowering Women,* the point she most emphasized about forgiving our parents was that they may not deserve it. That is just the point. Some don't. It isn't for **them.** You must forgive them in order that **you** may experience inner peace. Then you can open to joy and bliss, and then you can be healed. You just can't move on with your life until you let it all go. Louise has shared her personal, tragic story. She endured a horrible childhood. She referred to her parents as monsters. However, as she calmly spoke of this terrible time in her early life, she appeared to be at peace with it. She sat there, a vibrant and beautiful woman, who has positively affected the lives of millions. She could not have done this remarkable work, if she had not gone back and painfully worked through the issues. Step by step until it is healed, we must each deal with our own personal history.

Technique/Process:

"The Forgiveness Process"

"How many times must I forgive my brother?"

The Biblical answer is seventy times seven. One of my teachers suggested that we write this exercise seventy times for seven days in a row. Using your name begin:

> "*I, Georgia, love and forgive Daddy*
> *completely.*
> *You, Georgia, love and forgive Daddy*
> *completely.*
> *She, Georgia, loves and forgives Daddy*
> *completely.*"

Continue until you have written seventy sentences. Leave space for a response column. Write down whatever comes up for you during the exercise. Repeat the process daily for seven days. Many authors and psychologists recommend this process with variations. This particular one worked for me. Because my father was such a dear, sweet, wonderful person; it was not until the fifth day of the seven-day process that I realized there were a few items left unresolved. My dad was dependable, strong, loving and calm. He was a big, handsome man who worked hard, was faithful to my mother and loved us all. But, there on day five some human qualities and frailties came to my conscious mind. Big deal? No, but it was necessary to clear my past. Daddy died when I was twenty years old and I had to forgive him for leaving me. This is normal, *Psychology 101* material.

Be diligent and go with it. It works. After all is healed with one parent, move on to the other significant adult in your life. If you, like Louise Hay, have had a horrible childhood; repeat the process until the response column is empty. That will be your clue. You have healed the past and you are restored. You are ready to love and accept other human beings into your life with openness and trust.

Affirmation:

It is safe to love and be loved.
I forgive myself and all other beings.

The Past Is Over-- You Can Change It

Let's just suppose you were the bad guy in a past scenario. There may be a part of your life about which you are ashamed. What if you could change that? What if you could play it over? You have grown. You have matured. You have done your homework on personal transformation. The "new you" would be better and kinder and truer. There is a higher level of integrity and wisdom you have attained.

The idea here is to *change the past*. You are saying, "I don't think so, Ms. Shakti-Hill!" Okay, okay. Bear with me on this one. I know you might think that I am being silly and the past cannot be changed. Consider this: We are the directors of our movies. We are the authors of our books. What if we change the script? What if we just choose to rewrite a chapter? Let's create the best possible story with the happiest of all endings.

Technique/Process:

"Changing the Past"

Rewrite the story. Sit at the word processor or pick up pen and paper. Take back the words you wish had never been spoken. Remove a scene you wish had never been played. It can heal the experience. It can be that simple. Your intention to create a more harmonious past is enough to change the *energy* of the experience.

Next Step: You may begin thinking of your present situation as a movie. If you are the director, you may decide to remove a couple of current players. Perhaps, there are some people who do not support you and your highest good. You may not want them in your movie. Choose again. Heal the past. My friends and I were walking around reminding each other, "This isn't going to happen in my movie. I don't want him in *my* movie!" It is a fun new way to experience your personal power. There will be more about this in the next chapter.

Affirmation:

I release the past.

Words of Wisdom:

"There are no victims, only volunteers."

Humility and Worth

Robert Hudson is the author of *The Center of the Wheel*. In his chapter on humility and worth he wrote these beautiful thoughts:

> *"Realize that in the eyes of eternity,*
> *you cannot increase*
> *or decrease your worth.*

Your worth is constant.

Nothing you do,
good or bad,
can change that."

Robert is a sweet, gentle Spirit. I enjoyed our interview. I recommend his novel. He gave us permission to share some of his thoughts. My favorite message he shared in his book is this one:

"You are right where you belong.
Let go of your doubts and fears,
and
trust the process."

Freedom comes when we are able to see life differently. We move out of the victim mentality into empowerment. We are not the victims of our past. We are actually a powerful product of it. There has been a test and we have passed. There was trial by fire and we have come through as the victors. We would not have the depth of character we have attained, if the challenges had not been faced and met. Our past has served us well. It has made us strong and powerful. What can the future hold for us? Let's *Create the Future.*

♡ Chapter 2 ♡

Create the Future

I am often referred to as the "Oprah of southwest Florida." I always laugh and thank the person comparing me to this beloved American icon. She has served so many, so well, for so long; it is a true compliment. And behind my smile, there is a story. Remember the wonderful truism:

"Be very careful what you ask for . . .
you may get it."

I belong to an old and prestigious service organization, Pilot International. Our club was meeting one summer evening at a member's home. Our president-elect asked us to participate in one of those "getting to know you better" activities. We paired up and each of us was to answer a list of questions that would reveal secret information about ourselves. One query that would change my life was: "If you could choose a different profession, what might it be?"

Some of the answers from my Pilot sisters included giggles and then one mentioned an astronaut, another a musician. Some were silly. I clearly stated, "I would love to have been a television talk show host, like Oprah Winfrey. You can tell she loves what she is doing and it would be so easy for me to interview and chat with guests. And I have to admit, according to today's newspaper, she earned $30,000,000 this year. That's appealing!" We all chuckled and went on with our other socializing activities. That was the summer of 1991 and five months later in December, I became a local television talk show host. My journey to serve others and *Share the Light* began. As the new millennium nears, Oprah openly emphasizes a spiritual dimension to all of her programs. The Universe is ready and television is a powerful medium to communicate the message. (Incidentally, the $30 million still eludes me, however. Oprah's income this year is reported to be $125 million. Is this the Universal Law of Abundance manifesting as her reward for service?)

Empowerment--You Are Responsible for Your Future

Once you have released the pain from the past and forgiven all of the key players in your life, move on to your highest and your best! The next step I refer to is "taking back your power." It is a step that must be taken by each of us on the Path. The real question in this empowerment phase of our growth is to figure out to whom did we give away our power. Who has been our decision maker, who has made our choices for us? How many people negate our ideas and desires? Remember, you have left the victim mentality behind. Nobody is *doing it* to you any more without your knowledge and your permission. You are responsible. They don't get to vote on your life decisions. You can't blame them anymore. You choose it, you live it, you be it!

Technique/Process:

"The Power of Your Words"

I interviewed Robert Tennyson Stevens, author of the *Language of Mastery*. He teaches that we can be empowered through language consciousness. He asks us to use words of power such as these:

I am, I can, I will, I choose, I decide, I create.

Leave out *want* and *need*. They are self-defeating.
Pay attention to your choice of language.
Consciously empower yourself with a precise and
positive vocabulary.

Decision-Making

There is no tricky new process to learn on this
one. Just decide, decide, decide. Make one decision
after another. Start with the easy ones. Choose
where you are going to have dinner. Decide between
strawberry and chocolate. Don't just go shopping,
do some buying. Even if you make a mistake or two
and you appear to be wrong occasionally, practice
choosing over and over again. Change any part of
you or your life that had been dictated by someone
else. Next, move on to the big choices. Choose a
new career. Move to a new city. It is a muscle to be
exercised. The decision making muscle gets stronger
and you become empowered. It is your life. Own it!
Do it! Choose it!

Process/Technique:

"The Muktananda's Method"

The Muktananda was the founder of the Siddha Yoga movement, an international organization dedicated to bringing people to a state of bliss and peace and balance. While living in Newport Beach, California, I participated in the meditations and gatherings at the Siddha Center in Costa Mesa. My friend Erin shared with me the Muktananda's philosophies and served as my mentor. I asked her once about how I might decide a very difficult issue. She told me these are the three questions you ask yourself regarding any decision to be made:

> *Is it true to my nature?*
> *Will it make me happy?*
> *Is it what I really want to do?*

It is the simplicity of the questions that make them profound. The great Guru taught that it is not selfish to adhere to these answers. Perhaps there are times when you are the only person to be satisfied. Perhaps, you think you are choosing correctly for another person and you cannot choose for them. You might make everyone miserable. If you can be true to your nature, you have learned to trust yourself. If you are happy in your decision, you will proceed with power. If you have chosen with your mind and your heart, you will be successful!

Words of Wisdom:

"Not to decide, is to decide."

Affirmation:

I have the power to choose peace.

Being Happy--A Positive Mental Attitude

My husband has told me one of my best attributes is my happiness. Being happy is a characteristic that can be learned. It feels so much better to be laughing than crying. Smiling beats frowning. Love wins over fear. Choosing happiness is a conscious mental decision that is made over and over again. When confronted with a negative situation, our power lies in our ability to deal with the circumstances. Our response is what we control. One of life's greatest lessons is that we cannot control anyone else's behavior. We have no control over another person. We must realize and acknowledge our true power is in controlling our response to our own life's events. I took classes from Reverend Terry Cole-Whittaker in southern California. She taught us that we don't have the right to bring a dark cloud with us when we venture out into the world. Do not even leave your house until you have come back to joy. Sharing your negativity and depression with others is a major NO-NO! You can share your smile and your Light instead. When I am in front of audiences and remind them of this principle, they always laugh, applaud and look guilty. Yes! Choose happiness! It rings true.

Words of Wisdom:

"Do not leave your home with a dark cloud of negativity hanging over your head."
--Rev. Terry Cole-Whittaker

Technique/Process:

"The Power of A Smile"

Smiling is an interesting technique to use in most difficult situations. If someone with whom you are upset smiles at you in a genuine manner, it is disarming. I learned the power of the "smiling technique" from Angela Passidomo Trafford, author of *The Heroic Path* and *Remembering the Language of God.* She was one of my first guests on my television show years ago. She smiled at me during the entire one hour interview. An endless smile of joy and bliss was on her face. I realized how incredibly powerful it was to have that continual positive reinforcement. I consciously smiled at all of my guests throughout each interview from that point forward. It has become a natural part of me through the years. Countless guests have remarked how comfortable they are with me, because of my smile. It is sincere. I appreciate so much their sharing their wisdom and their Light with me and my audience. It makes me smile.

A Natural State of Being

One of my associates mentioned that she could not believe how I am always smiling. She said she has watched me walking along the beach alone with a smile on my face. She has seen me in the grocery store shopping with a look of bliss. She asked how can anyone be that happy? I reminded her that *happiness is the natural state of being.* Large corporations train their employees to answer the phone with a smile. The person on the other end of the line can *feel* it. When I am angry with someone (and, yes, that still happens), I envision them and put a smile on my face . . . no matter how difficult it seems. Eventually, I can actually master the positive feeling and the anger subsides. The energy behind a smile is contagious. Go ahead and grin!

Humor and Bernie Siegel, M.D.

When I introduced Dr. Bernie Siegel to our television audience, I said he could have been a doctor or a stand-up comic. The man uses humor in healing, and has done so with great success for many years. He was a pioneer in this concept. His books and tapes are a study in the power of love and joy. Bernie entertains, as he teaches. In his best-selling book, *Love, Medicine and Miracles,* Dr. Siegel explains the power of love and laughter in healing. In our interview for "Living in Balance" he shared one humorous story after another from patients with the right kind of attitude--the attitude that allowed healing to take place physically and spiritually.

Words of Wisdom:

"Joy is the most infallible sign of the presence of God."
--Teilhard de Chardin

Dealing with Anger and Upset

Sometimes it takes more than a smile. Sometimes the world seems very harsh. Life has dealt you a cruel blow. Bouncing back to bliss is not always an easy option. I remember when I was very young and I would become livid with anger or feel a deep emotional upset. My whole body changed. It felt like a chemical reaction was taking place. I hated being mad. I hated being so sad. I later found out that a chemical reaction *was* taking place. When I began teaching stress management in seminars, the scientific data I shared explained the body's physiological response. There are great health dangers in allowing that level of anger and upset. You pay a heavy toll and it is your mind that can get you back to balance. What is the first step toward peace?

Process/Technique:

"The Witness State" or
"Be in the world, but not of it"

An effective technique is to step back and go into "the witness state." Pretend once again that you are watching a movie. The central player in the drama is you. To see this clearly, your role must shift and you must become a member of the audience. You can be a <u>very interested</u> audience member, as you are watching your scenario unfold. As an uninvolved observer of your life, you can objectively view the event. Edgar Cayce referred to it as learning patience and tolerance. Now the power comes in your ability to analyze, reflect and choose the best response. Taking the emotion and upset out of the equation allows your mind to do its best work. Sometimes I feel bad for Georgia Shakti-Hill, because I know this is a tough one for her to handle. At some level she *always* knows exactly what to do. That inner knowing comes from experience. And, we can allow our wisdom to shine through, if we remove our emotions from the picture. She wants to choose peace. She wants to come back to balance. She can.

Prima Donna is a Mirror

I recently interviewed a woman, and we will lovingly refer to her as, Prima Donna. She made the entire crew, staff and audience wait for her arrival. She was late. She walked in the door, not yet dressed for the camera. We all waited while she changed her clothes. She completed the interview and wanted to start over. She sang her song and completed her performance and wanted to review it and then change it. No one wanted her on the set. They couldn't wait to get rid of her. No one wanted to redo, repeat or revisit Miss Donna. She is wonderfully talented and she evoked rejection from all who worked with her. Only one calm and truly evolved Old Soul had enough patience in this situation. The tough ones are our "mirrors." She reminded me that the *Ego* can lead us down the wrong path. I heard someone say that she was *too high maintenance.* One of our crew came up to me and said, "Please don't ever be like her no matter how successful you become. You don't want to be the Prima Donna." Look at the people that upset you, as if they are your mirrors. Ask for the lessons that they are teaching you in every difficult situation. Our Prima Donna taught us a great lesson, a great reminder!

Affirmations:

I am the director of my movie.
I am imaginative and productive.
People want to be in my presence.

I create bliss!

Visualization--Hold That Thought

If you have not experienced your own power to create your life as you desire it, wow, are you in for an awesome surprise! What you can make happen in your life, will astound you. That is why the old adage, *"Be very careful what you ask for . . . you may get it"* is so profound. The ability to manifest is true to your nature. The clearer you are as a channel of Universal Light, the faster the results come to you. A stage in your evolvement is to practice visualizing what you want and then getting it. Bill Turner, founder of The Wisdom Channel, told me that he had held the vision of a network dedicated to healing and spirituality. It had been his dream for fifteen years. He had thought it, he had desired, he had created it in his mind. He shared his vision with people of like mind around him. When the time was right, the Wisdom Channel came into being. Then it became the Wisdom Network. He now broadcasts positive programming 24 hours a day on both television and radio. Our program airs on Wisdom.

Andrea de Michaelis

Andrea de Michaelis, publisher of *Horizon Magazine*, was a recent guest on our series called "Women of Vision." She explained how easy it is to manifest abundance in your life. She suggests it is as simple as make-believe and fantasizing. She teaches that all you have to do is create it in your mind with power and conviction and it will happen in life! She is successful and living proof of that principle.

Audrey Craft Davis

One of our *Friends* that you will meet later in our second book, *Sharing the Wisdom and Light,* Audrey Craft Davis, is wonderful. She wrote *Metaphysical Techniques that Really Work.* Audrey shared with us these thoughts:

"We are all magnetic poles. We attract the people and situation in accordance with our thinking. If we are positive, we attract positive people and circumstances. If we are negative, we attract negative persons and situations. Like attracts like."

In each chapter she explains how you can use this profound power that you have to achieve success in your life. She shares the basics of visualization and empowerment.

Technique/Process:

"Visualization"

There are a lot of qualifiers here that must be considered. You must ask for the *highest and the best* for all concerned. You must ask for *this or something better*. What you consider to be your good, should harm no other. You must be specific, clear and direct. Declare the exact time, color, size, the destination, a specific amount, etc. Consider yourself the artist and your painting must be detailed. Be as precise as you can be. Use qualifiers whether you are asking for a soul mate or a Jaguar or good health. Create the picture. Hold the vision.

Affirmations:

In this situation I ask for the highest and the best for all concerned.
I ask for this or something better.

After healing our past and looking to the future, we have the power to create our lives as we desire them. We can be open to our highest and our best. We can leave behind the pain and visualize our goals and aspirations, as if they were already accomplished. We can exclude the dark and welcome the Light. We can awaken our power within. It is our Divine right. No one has the power or the ability to block us. It is our purpose and our responsibility to move along our Path. The next assignment is to *Surrender to Success*!

♡ Chapter 3 ♡

Surrender to Success

After releasing the pain of your past and imagining the best possible future, it is now time to *surrender* to the Divine. You've become a clear channel and you've released all negativity. You can open to the full flow of abundance. You can get out of the way, let go and let God. You can allow Divine intervention. How will you know, if you are on the right Path? How will you know, if you have visualized your highest and your best? It will all begin to fall into place. Luck will be on your side. Destiny will unfold before your eyes. You won't have to *effort* to such a degree. You will be required, however, to *surrender* to your highest and your best. You will have to get out of the way of your life and allow it to happen.

A premise that you will need to accept is that you may not know what is best for you. In the last chapter I asked you to take back your power. Now I'm asking you to turn over your power to a Higher Power. I like to refer to the process as allowing Divine intervention to work its miracles in my life. I like to refer to it as the Universe supporting my endeavors. I measure my success by the flow of abundance in my life. I define this abundance as bliss, peace, happiness and health *and wealth*. That is measurable. If you are trying and trying and not succeeding, choose again. You have simply chosen the wrong endeavor. Failure is your teacher. Failure is your gift of awareness from the Universe. If you don't know how to succeed, there are experts and professionals in the field to help you along your Path. I've interviewed several excellent teachers.

Success is the Journey

Wally Amos is a wise and wonderful teacher of success and failure. He shared his wisdom and his Light in his book, *Watermelon Magic--Seeds of Wisdom, Slices of Life*. His story is powerful in that he created a vast empire on a chocolate chip cookie. He has ability in many varied professions. He is a talented man. He said he thought of himself as a cookie. When the cookie crumbled, Wally experienced temporary defeat. He tells how he picked himself up and got back in the race! He realized, success is not the destination, *success is the journey*.

Dr. Cynthia Adams

Dr. Cynthia Adams, success therapist, described this process in working with athletes or companies. She asks you to release the blocks from your past experiences. She counsels that you don't allow other people or events to take up space in your thoughts. Choose to do the positive and be your own best friend. Believe in something and be very clear on your own value system. Finally, you must accept that you *deserve* to be successful. Her work as a counselor with individuals and companies has had powerfully positive results. When I interviewed her on "Living in Balance" about success, she said the challenge is often to *continue* being on top. She suggests you nurture the "fun" part of your endeavor. Always keep learning and challenging yourself with new adventures and ideas. Continue to remember that you are a spiritual being and acknowledge there is a power within you that is greater than the physical and the mental.

Al Oerter

Al Oerter, the four-time Olympic gold medalist and record setting athlete, joined us in the discussion. Al continued with the philosophy of goal setting, desire, hard work. He emphasized emotional acceptance of accomplishment, higher goals, more hard work. There is no room here for self-defeating behaviors. Mentally and physically you focus. When the body can't do it, the mind takes over and you go on, because you have set a goal. Spirit has a role that Al said cannot be defined, but can be experienced. He gives motivational talks to groups and corporations all over the country. Al Oerter is a success scenario and true winner!

Technique/Process:

"Let the Universe Decide"

Create a cassette recording of your favorite positive thoughts or affirmations. Include phrases that fit into your personal spiritual philosophy like:

" Let Go and Let God. I turn this over to Higher Power for my highest and my best.

Let the Universe decide. I surrender and allow. Show me the truth in this."

A Paradigm of Success

Dr. Lois Bolin is one of our *Friends* you will meet in our second book *Sharing the Wisdom and Light.* Her company is called "Success Fulfillment" and she, too, counsels businesses in their steps to prosperity. She wrote:

"Incorporating spirituality into our daily work life is considered *new paradigm thinking.* In the new paradigm, life is seen as a *whole* and all of life is connected in some form or fashion. Conversely, *old paradigm thinking* discounts this interconnectedness theme and views spirituality and business as *separate,* incompatible concerns."

This new paradigm of success must begin with a mission statement and a vision statement. You can't know if you have accomplished your goals, if you haven't set them. You must have a guiding light that directs you on your Path.

Technique/Process:

"My Vision Statement"

Whether you are a business or an individual, you need to clarify what you wish to attain. I have always found that being required to write it down, to formulate it in words, has required me to focus and be concise and aware. To write it, I must know it. The mastery is in the completion of the task. Create your own vision statement. Put it on the wall for all to see. My mother sent me a cookbook when we opened up our little gourmet coffee shop. She used an expression from the Greek culture usually reserved for artists: *hands of gold*. She wished me "hands of gold" in my endeavor. I was moved by the beauty of the phrase and created this thought:

" God grant us hands of gold that we may nourish all who enter here.
God bless us all with inner peace that we may share our Love."

We engaged a calligrapher to pen a beautiful rendition of the verse, and it hung over our tiny kitchen for all to see. It was our reminder of why we had started this business, especially when we were overwhelmed, tired and being tested! I can't tell you the number of customers who commented on the plaque through the years. It was our vision statement.

Our mission statement was simple. We had chosen to create a successful gourmet cafe. Our goal was to allow abundance to flow to us, as we satisfied our customers' needs by serving high quality, tasty food in a pleasant and beautiful atmosphere. It was sweet and simple!

Affirmation:

Abundance flows to me and through me in Divine Order.

Words of Wisdom:

"Success is the Journey, not the destination."

Achieving True Success

Gary Moore is one of our *Friends* who is sharing his wisdom in our second book. He has given us permission to reprint the tenth rule from his book, *Ten Golden Rules for Financial Success:*

"Measure success with a single word--**love**."

Sir John Templeton has been Gary's mentor and guiding light. They share a philosophy of responsible investing and stewardship. You will enjoy this fascinating and refreshing perspective from Wall Street to spirituality. The biblical influence in finances is interesting.

Words of Wisdom:

"I have come that you might have life and have it more abundantly."
--John 10:10.

Trust

Dr. Lee Jampolsky has written a book on trust. As I sat and interviewed him about the idea of personal growth, he said we need to learn to trust ourselves, our own inner knowing. Many people refer to this as our intuition, our inner guide to our highest and best. Some believe we are tapping into Infinite Intelligence. Many seem to agree at some level we *do* know what is best for us. We must learn to trust our instincts. It is metaphorically a muscle that needs exercised. If we choose correctly, the Universe supports us. We have the perfect flow of abundance in our lives . . . and we are in balance! We have chosen correctly.

Deepak Chopra, M.D. and Balance

In an interview with Dr. Chopra at the Chopra Center for Well Being in La Jolla, California, I asked him about the balance between mind, body and spirit. He explained:

"Whatever happens to the body affects the mind. Whatever happens to the mind affects the body. The

two are inseparably one. They are not just connected. They are both an expression of the Spirit. . . ."

How beautifully he expressed that thought. His worldwide success in bringing this philosophy to others indicates the Universe supports his work. His messages resonate and others find truth in his wisdom.

So it is in this *"trilogy of Light"* that the mind plays its role. If we can heal, control, educate and train our minds; we can harness that power and energy to serve us well. It is part of that triad of balance of mind, body, Spirit. It is with our minds we release the pain of the past, create the most perfect future and surrender to success. Now we can move onto "Living in Balance" with our body and Spirit! Are you ready to *Heal the Body?*

Section II "Body"

♡ Chapter 4 ♡

Heal the Body

Irecently had a terrible toothache. It was an extremely rare experience for me and I waited to see if it would simply go away. It persisted for a couple days. I was preparing for a trip to Scottsdale and Sedona, Arizona. I reluctantly realized that the dentist must be visited. Of course, waiting for a lengthy time was part of the indignity of visiting the traditional medical facility. I have not, yet, mastered patience as a virtue. I am consciously working on this attribute. So, I was taking advantage of the "down time" by reading one more of John Randolph Price's books. John is a prolific author and I was immersed in his writings in preparation for our Scottsdale interview. I admit I was doing some speed reading and quickly perusing *Practical Spirituality*. As my eyes dashed across a quotation for healing, my mind sped on then came to a screeching halt! "Stop! Return to that quotation," a little voice whispered within. I went back and intently reread the following words of wisdom:

"The forgiving, cleansing love of Christ now frees me from all negative thoughts and emotions. I turn within and open the door to the River of Life and let the healing currents flow through me. I am purified and vitalized with this Christ Life within. I am renewed according to the perfect pattern of Spirit. God sees me as well, complete, vibrant, strong and perfect. And, so I am."

At that instant the pain went away. I reread the quote. The pain was instantly gone. I smiled to myself, called the dental assistant and told her I was leaving. My 45-minute wait had ended with a healing. I cautiously tested the area of my mouth for pain throughout that day and the next. It was gone. One of my favorite quotes from *A Course in Miracles* came to mind:

"Healing takes place the instant you give up the value of the pain."

The Body is a Temple

We have been taught our bodies are our temples. Some have written that our bodies' only purposes are as vessels to carry around our Souls. *ACIM* teaches,

"I am not a body, I am free. I am as God created me."

And, we must honor this body and care for it as a holy vessel. We can measure our mental and spiritual and emotional health through the health of the body.

Pain Burns Karma

I have found that nothing takes precedence over a body in pain and disease. It gets our attention and demands relief or at least action. Pain is humbling. It is a great teacher. A Burmese Buddhist monk, the Venerable U Vimala, taught that all disease is karmic. He was my teacher for a while and Bhante, as he has been affectionately called, taught that the karma can be from this life or a past life. He taught the comforting thought that pain burns karma. I have shared that lesson with a few people in great pain. It has encouraged their resolve to endure for a higher purpose.

I loved interviewing U Vimala. He would bring all of the visiting monks with him to participate on our television show. They would come into the studio bowing and smiling, dressed in their saffron robes. They would happily join us on the set. It mattered not that they spoke no English. They sat proudly, looking very wise and loving. Bhante had been brought to our area by two doctors. They had established a temple for their children and community to be taught the language and the principles of the Buddha. This Florida temple was very popular for the other monks to visit, especially in winter. Bhante had all the knowledge of the healers. He had teas and herbs and tonics. He taught the *kindness meditation blessing*. I've adapted it to meet the positive language criteria. I still repeat it almost every day of my life. Bhante has left this plane. His joy and wisdom remain in the hearts and minds of his students.

Technique/Process:

"The Kindness Meditation"

"May I be well, happy and peaceful. May I be safe and meet with success. May my husband be well, happy and peaceful. May he be safe and meet with success . . . may my mother . . . may my friends . . . may my teachers . . . may my kittens . . . etc. May all beings be well, happy and peaceful. May they be safe and may they meet with success."

The Muktananda's Mantra:

"Om Namah Shivaya"

This is the Guru's mantra. It translates to "I bow to Shiva." But, it refers to the power of God within each of us. It is the higher Self. It is the boundless love within each of us and it is all-powerful. When one bows to another person and repeats the mantra, it is as if you are honoring the God-spark within the other person. It is as if you are saying, "The God-spark within me honors the God-spark within you." It is the spiritual equivalent of shaking hands in the most reverent of manners. I repeat the mantra as a chant of protection and balance and love. I use it to change my vibration or the vibration of my circumstance. It is taught in the Siddha philosophy that repeating the mantra connects you to the great Guru, the Muktananda. You can dissolve karma and share the benefits of his enlightenment. Its very power is awakened by your awareness of the purpose of chanting. Because it has been repeated over and over by millions of people, you can click into the essence of all that power and energy and love and wisdom.

Words of Wisdom:

"God dwells within you as you."
                                        --*Swami Muktananda*

These are great mantras to use as you drive down life's roads and freeways. They certainly set a kindness mode for the day. If I am worried about someone, The Kindness Meditation helps alleviate the anxiety for them. "Om Namah Shivaya" is a universal chant of grace-bestowing power.

Nourish the Body

Now let's talk about this body and keeping it healthy. Nutrition is of greatest importance. I am a pesco-vegetarian. True veggies would scoff at the term. It means I still eat fish or seafood once or twice a week. . A true vegetarian does not include any animal products: no eggs, milk, cheese, cream, butter . . . NONE! They eat fruits, vegetables, nuts, legumes. The pesco approach works for me. My husband is a "meat and potatoes" guy. I love to cook and I feed him well. I've designated cooking as a hobby. I asked Eddie at one point, "How important is eating to you?"

He looked at me as if I had truly lost my mind. He cautiously and bluntly replied, "It is **VERY** important to me." Because it takes so much time to cook from scratch and with some style, I designated the culinary arts as a hobby. I could then justify spending an hour or two a day in the kitchen. To keep Eddie healthy I add at least five vegetables or fruits to his meat and potatoes.

Becoming a Vegetarian

The vegetarian lifestyle is not a judgment on my part. It has not been a philosophical decision completely. I feel *lighter* and to me that is better. It began with letting hamburger go and then all beef-- pork--chicken--and it was easy. There is a philosophical aspect to my thought process, I must admit. I just feel better about not eating cows, chickens, turkeys and pigs.

I had a friend who told the story of befriending a pig. The relationship resulted in her becoming a vegetarian. She was visiting her daughter. The daughter had purchased a pig. Each evening just before dusk my friend would go to a grassy knoll and sit and watch the sun set. The pig joined her every night. They sat together in appreciation of the beauty and grandeur of the sky. They communed in silence. They bonded. When the time came to "butcher the hog," it was too gruesome and barbaric a thought. To eat her gentle companion was unconscionable. She became an instant veggie.

I grow my own vegetables . . . another hobby. They are organic, of course. The herbicides and pesticides scare me. Do your best on this issue. Rinse all your vegetables and fruits thoroughly. Buy organic produce where and when you can. Find a local farmer or communal garden, if you have no space to grow. My garden is only about 14' X 14'. I am able to include tomatoes, peppers, onions, eggplant, mustard, broccoli, sweet potatoes, cauliflower, collards, carrots, radishes, brussels sprouts and I have a small herb garden, too. It gives me great pleasure. It grounds me and I even chat with the plants. There is a statue of an angel that overlooks the garden and another angel for the herbs, too. Of all the activities in my life, gardening is one I would choose to spend more time doing.

Phyllis Balch and Nutritional Healing

Phyllis Balch is one of my frequent guests. She has coauthored the world's best selling book on nutrition, *Prescription for Nutritional Healing*. It is a great reference book. I highly recommend it. I suggest you give it to everyone you love. Phyllis spent sixteen years in the original research for the book. It was recently revised and put out in a small paperback version to carry to the health food store. She has done your work for you. Look up any illness and she has written what nutrients, herbs, teas and behaviors are required to come back to wellness.

Technique/Process:

"Dr. Green on Greens"

Dr. Steven Green is a dentist with a passion for nutrition. He told my television audience that they could improve their health in one easy step. Add two cups of greens to the daily diet and there would be profound and incredible results. He said four cups would double the reward. It could be lettuce, peas, broccoli, beans; just make it *green . . . the greener the better.* He also observed that the health of the body was reflected in the mouth. Periodontal disease was an indicator or precursor to heart disease, etc. Dr. Green calls his practice and his book *Eclectic Dentistry.*

Wellness

I have learned the body and its level of wellness is reflective of our mental and spiritual health. *Dis-ease* is a result of being out of balance. It is the perfect indicator of how we are living and loving ourselves. Are we being true to our nature? When I have not made decisions for my own best interests, I have paid a very heavy price. Going against your nature and your true desires wreaks havoc on the body. Twice I have gone "under the knife." I consider surgery to be necessary when we have failed our bodies. Bless the medical doctors for coming to our aid. Shame on us for requiring it. Stress is a factor in all illnesses. I believe it is the decisive factor. The body could have coped with the bacteria or the virus or the condition had we kept it in balance. So, the body is our greatest teacher of how well we are living in balance. The Lord of Karma is simply cause and effect.

Words of Wisdom:

" As you sow, so shall you reap."

Kaye Cude, Angel of the Garden

One of the most beautiful beings I have had the pleasure of interviewing is the Angel of the Garden, Kaye Cude. She has authored a book on herbs, and is a teacher of *A Course in Miracles*. She listens to the plants and cares for them accordingly. She also teaches us to listen to our bodies, as they can be our teachers. Kaye has expressed this principle so well. She says that we are not being tested with a disease. We have simply strayed away from *peace*. An illness indicates a change in the lifestyle is required, not just a prescription, not just the surgery. We need a change in lifestyles. The more serious the illness, the greater the change necessary.

Addictions (Have to mention them)

Give them up. Lee Jampolsky, Ph.D. told me we are all addicted to something, if we have a need outside of ourselves. We must ask what or who do we require to make us happy. On what or whom is our happiness dependent? Build your inner peace and you can allow the addictions to be healed. Own it, bless it and let it go.

I smoked two-and-a-half packs of cigarettes a day. I never attempted to stop, because I knew I couldn't. The Universe sent me messages in synchronicity. I was in a business meeting with a man who said he could no longer smoke. He wished he could. However, he had been hypnotized and he was no longer *able* to smoke. That statement got my attention. The next day I met another nonsmoker who praised the same person for helping her quit the habit. I quietly contacted the hypnotherapist that both people had mentioned. I found her and had one session and one follow-up visit for encouragement. That was August 28, 1981. She told me I was an addict and I could never have another cigarette. I haven't. I couldn't go moderately on with my habit. I was not able to cut down. Moderation is the indicator of your successful release of an addictive behavior. If you are not ready to do something in moderation, the other option is to quit. When I gave up the tobacco, I felt so powerful; I knew I could do anything. My self-esteem soared. In that feeling of power I found peace.

I occasionally go out of balance with my weight and I do not want to be even moderately obese, nor chubby. Neither of those descriptions feels good. Therefore, I must exercise self-control and remind myself,

"I am the master of my body. And, I choose to be thin"

Affirmations:

I am a powerful, spiritual being and I choose a healthy body.

I love and accept my body.
Every day in every way I'm getting better
and better.
I have a thin and healthy body.

Healers I Have Met

I told you earlier that I had survived a serious surgery in 1983. It included my going for a second then third and then fourth opinion. There was a possibility I had cancer. They wouldn't know until the surgery was complete. This so frightened me, I chose to take a journey of discovery in healing. First approach was a blessing of the peacock feather by the guru in Santa Monica. I had a visit from the Mexican *curanderisma,* who had healed my hairdresser's mom. Prayers from the elders of a Pentecostal church and a *laying on of hands* came next. The hypnotherapist sent little "pac men" after the diseased cells. At that point I was ready to submit to the knife. I chose an East Indian doctor whose philosophy was *simpatico* to mine. He told me he believed we were just passing through this life. He told me, if I did not have the surgery; I would just pass through faster. I was operated on and there was no cancer. Might there have been before all of those healers worked their magic on me? We will never know. It was a journey I had to take.

Words of Wisdom:

"Your faith has made you well; go in peace, and be healed of your disease."

--*Mark 5:34*

In the Company of Healers

Now, I am in the company of healers all the time. One incident was so profound that I will share it with you. We had a gathering at our little cafe on the beach. Rev. Richard Smith was teaching a class on healing. Richard is a minister and the head of the Center of Eternal Light. He was demonstrating a technique called MariEL with a woman in the class. She had abdominal pain. We watched him moving his hands up and down her energy field without actually touching her body. I was sitting off to the side and intently observing the action. I began to see little light beams coming from her body to his hand.

As he moved his hands backward and forward, I could see lines of lightning-like energy emanating from her abdomen to his right palm. His left hand was behind her back. I was astounded. She was relieved of pain. It was a fascinating experience. There were many more to come with other gentle Souls intent on healing those in need.

I considered listing some of the fabulous healers that, I have interviewed for our talk show. "Living in Balance." So many people have the passion and feel the direction to serve others in coming back to health. An entire book would be necessary to share with you all of the wonderful people who have dedicated their lives to bringing others to balance and wellness. One attribute that all of the healers I have interviewed possess, is they know they are not the healers. They are the facilitators who create the space for people to do their own healing. They are channels of love and Light, who allow the power to move through them. They each express it differently and with different terminology. Rev. Richard Smith describes himself as jumper cables, just connecting someone to God's healing love. Bottom line: they are conduits of healing. Call us or send an e-mail, if you would like to be in touch with a healer.

I have been trained as a Reiki Master. Reiki is a

type of "laying on of hands." It includes absentee healing and incorporates a series of symbols. It is ancient and it is effective. Handed down from Master to student, only recently to be divulged in print. Some experts say power is dissipated by allowing people who are not serious students to know the secrets. That is an age-old dilemma that goes back to the great shamans and the Kabbalah and the Tibetan oral teachings. I do not know the answer here. We each must ponder and decide. I chose to learn a systematic approach to sharing the power of healing with thousands of years of tradition. Robert Archer, a naturopath in Sedona, Arizona, said his teachers gave him two criteria for healing techniques. If the technique is at least three thousand years old and used on three continents, you can trust it. I agree. Once you have healed your body, you are ready to keep it healthy. So, let's *Move the Body!*

♡ **Chapter 5** ♡

Move the Body

I live on a barrier island with the Gulf of Mexico as my neighbor. A friend and I began walking the beach in January of 1990. It might have been the proverbial New Year's Resolution. I don't recall. One day I realized I hadn't seen the beach for a month. Of course, the beach was one of the reasons I had chosen to live on Estero Island when I moved to Florida. Working so hard and intently, my priorities had gotten totally out of whack. Teaching classes on spiritual development for four years had given me the opportunity to share what kept one in balance. I decided to literally *walk my talk*. We teach what we need most to learn. I knew the benefits of walking.

I want a thin and healthy body.

I want to release tension and commune with nature.

Negative ions from the gulf waters produce positive effects on the body.

Power walking firms the body and strengthens the lungs.

A hearty appetite is suppressed with walking.

When we vigorously exercise, the brain releases interferon and a natural high is experienced; a positive mental attitude results.

No equipment is necessary, just good walking shoes.

You can walk anytime, night or day, sunrise or sunset or midnight.

If you choose compatible partners, you can discuss or collaborate or share.

Walking alone is wonderful.

Creative thinking is enhanced.

My best ideas come to me, when I'm walking. On average I walk six days a week and I have given my body an opportunity to live longer with a higher quality of existence. We have acquired a second home in the mountains of North Carolina and that allows me to walk in the woods. God has been very good to me!

Technique/ Process:

"Power Walking"

Choose a friend or two. Three seems to work out better because someone is almost always available. Make a commitment to each other to set a pattern of walking that works with your schedule. Be diligent and dependable. Be flexible and accommodative, when you are able. Walk at least twenty minutes daily. Build up to an hour every day. Even if it has to be a *quickie*, a brief walk is better than no movement at all. Treat yourself to really good shoes. You are worth it and your feet will remain your friends. Walk at the fastest pace that allows you to carry on a conversation. Choose as natural an environment, as you can find. If you live in an area with severe winters, have an alternate plan to walk the mall or indoor arena.

Words of Wisdom:

"We teach what we need most to learn."

Tai Chi--Meditation in Motion

I love *tai chi*. I describe it as the ancient Chinese meditation in motion. I saw it once performed at sunrise on the shore of the Gulf of Mexico. Linda Townsend and Peter Anazone were honoring us at a festival of synchronicity at the time of the Harmonic Convergence in August of 1987. People had gathered to pray for peace and to open to the possibilities that all people on the planet could experience love. It had been prophesied by the Hopi Indians and foretold by the Mayans and their calendar, we could make a shift in consciousness on the Earth. It would require 144,000 *"rainbow teachers"* from all over the world to commit to changing their own consciousness. There was media hype and millions participated. Our beach community did its part. And, Linda and Peter were slow-moving dancers on the sand.   It was watching the *yin* and *yang* personified. As the sun rose, there was a fine haze upon the water giving a mystical quality to the movements. Beauty and power blended in a sacred and serene flow of energy. I became a reverent student of *tai chi*. It is a meditation in motion.

Master Lee

Master Lee of the *White Tiger School of Tai Chi* teaches the techniques to students who are ready to profess a desire for personal growth. He identified the most important qualities for the teachers of *tai chi* and *chi kung (*or *Qi gong)* in an interview on "Living in Balance." *Chi kung* is the breathing technique that enhances the power and the benefits of this discipline. To be an instructor in the high martial arts, Master Lee chooses people for their decency and strength of character. *Tai chi* and *chi kung* massage the internal organs and build power. The benefits are peace and power, tranquility and self-mastery. It is totally related to the entire Chinese and Asian philosophies of flow and balance, *yin* and *yang*, the *I Ching* and *feng shui* and *chi kung*.

Tom Baeli is an instructor of *tai chi* and *chi kung*. This man has devoted his life to these arts. He has been a guest on my program many times. Tom is a tough trainer. He rebukes the students, if they miss one day of practice. You must begin again at the beginning and it will take you 100 days to come back to the point when you missed. He is a serious task master and excellent teacher. This is a wonderful discipline for you to pursue, no matter what your age or physical condition. You will just get better and better!

Hatha Yoga and Stretching

"You are as young as your spine is flexible . . ." truer words were never spoken. Flexibility and poise are positive results of *hatha* yoga or stretching. The *asanas* or positions are named after nature--mountain pose, cobra, etc. Kandy Love is a teacher of the Iyengar method and has been my instructor on occasion and a frequent contributor to our program. There is a strong element of self-discipline here, too. The postures are basic. The techniques are precise. A good instructor will make you move your hip out just a fraction further to attain the correct stretch. When you are limber and flexible, you move with greater ease and flow. Your body is more nimble and graceful. I have seen *yogis* and *yoginis* (the female yogi) perform extreme postures that appear to be impossible for the human body. Although I love to watch them, those extreme configurations are simply not required of the student of yoga. Stretching every muscle of the body with a proper technique is the goal. Being limber and flexible is the reward. *Prana* is the breath and the life force, the Hindu equivalent of *chi*. Breathing techniques build power here, also. If you find a good teacher, you'll love yoga. A good stretch class will allow you to experience the relaxation and release of power.

Words of Wisdom:

"You are as young as your spine is flexible."

Technique/ Process:

"Nature's Stretch"

I have three Siamese cats. Leo, Mango and Dax are excellent instructors in the art of stretching. When they first awaken, they stretch before moving from their resting places. They gracefully move their bodies with gentle and yet extreme positions. They relax into the postures. They hold and then release.

They move back into the opposite direction. Animals are our teachers of the natural movements. Try moving like the feline and embrace the flow of your body!

Dance Like Nobody's Watching

I love to dance. It frees my Spirit. It allows me to be exactly who I am. If you have forgotten to dance lately, just do it. Turn on the tunes, hum a little song or choose a video. Take a class. Find a friend and dance! When I was nine years old, I knew I would have to choose between being a professional dancer or becoming a teacher, when I grew up. I chose teaching, and I kept on dancing. There is nothing more natural than a child dancing and whirling about in play. There is no movement more inherent to the human body than dancing. Every culture dances. Every country has their traditional dance. It is beautiful to watch, and fabulous to do. I took dance classes from the time I was a small child. I continued it as a hobby in my adulthood, and then I forgot to dance. At one point I realized I had neglected to dance. It had been years without the experience of freeing the Spirit as you flowed to the sounds of music or your own rhythm. It came about unexpectedly in a hypnotherapy session. A group of us gathered to have a session with Janet Cunningham, author of *A Tribe Returned.* I had just interviewed Janet for "Living in Balance" and, we thought it would be fun to have a group adventure. I had told you of my past success with quitting smoking through hypnosis. I had gotten out of balance again and wanted to lose weight. I asked Janet as my guiding question to take me to a past life that would give me insights on my body. She did. I went to a time when I had to give up all of the pleasures of life including dancing. It was in Egypt and I was being initiated as a Priestess. I had serious responsibilities and I could no longer dance and frolic and play. Okay, okay, maybe it was my vivid imagination! We may never know. Bottom line-- Janet reminded me to dance in this lifetime. I began taking Natural Movement Dance classes with J.J. Cochrane and Cathy Oerter. Natural Movement Dance was patterned after the style of Isadora Duncan, freeing the Spirit. The pounds melted off once again. Did dancing do it? It doesn't matter. Dancing was a part of my reclaiming my natural body. I remembered how much I loved the experience and danced and danced; at home and at class, I danced and danced.

Affirmation:

I love my body.

Gaia Lamb, the "Saint of Sedona"

On a recent trip to Sedona, Arizona, I interviewed Gaia Lamb. Sedonans lovingly referred to her as a "saint." She teaches a movement called *Body Bliss*. We walked and talked along the Oak Creek area, and I watched her communicating with the trees and rocks and animals through arm movements. I laughed and joined her as we danced with nature. It was fun, pure pleasure. I recaptured that feeling when I returned to our North Carolina retreat. While walking along a path in the woods, I began to lightly move and turn. My arms just naturally began to flow with the movement and I frolicked through the forest like a fairy. In fact I went to an area we refer to as the Fairy Ring and danced in the circle. Can you imagine my delight?

Words of Wisdom:

"Dance like nobody's watching."

Dancing--When in the Desert of Arabia

"He came to a high cliff where he felt that he could lift his arms and touch and feel the tender blue color of heaven. He was singing and felt his voice carry him with the echo to all the sand dunes."

So says the Sufi Master, Adnan Sirhan. I had the pleasure of interviewing the Sufi Master. He is with the International Sufi Association of America. Adnan teaches dance in the ancient Mediterranean style. He explains the power of dance brings you into the moment. You release all other thoughts and issues and cares and human concerns and you connect to the Divine. He expresses the connection as a pure instant in time when all else is gone. You are in the NOW. You are in the moment. You can reach bliss and peace! Adnan is one of our *Friends* and he has written a lovely chapter for our second book.

Solana and *Trance Dance*

Solana teaches *Trance Dance* and has traveled the world with her gift to share. As one of our *Friends*, she, too, shares a story later on with us. It is a tender tale and an incredibly intimate communication between her and her husband, who has passed over. Solana suggests you close your eyes, let the music move you and be one with the music. Drumming takes you to a deeper level of meditation. The music heals your body.   The experience is total and profound! You'll meet her in *Sharing the Wisdom and Light.*

Process/Technique:

"Drumming to Your Heartbeat"

Find a drum. Borrow a drum. Create a drum. Use any object that has a good vibration when you beat on it. Morgan Eaglebear, Apache Medicine Man, teaches drumming. LeRoy White is a drumming instructor and musician on a *Soul and Conscience Tour*. Each has shared classes in healing with the beat of a drum. Each has shared his drumming with our audiences.   Start with the rhythm of your own heartbeat. Continue with the heart's rhythm and allow it to become a part of you. Close your eyes and drum. Create the beat that you feel. Kokoman Clottey and his wife Aeeshah of the Attitudinal Healing Connection explained how they use the drum to bond with participants at their center. They drum for at least twenty minutes before they begin to share. Kokoman explains that there is a deeper level of intimacy and safety that is created with drumming. It crosses all cultural boundaries. It is true to our nature. Try it.

Words of Wisdom:

"We are the music. We are the sound."

"We know the dances of the Hopi hold the planet intact."

--Dhyani Ywahoo, Cherokee Teachings

As you have read, I love movement. When I am not moving, dancing, stretching, walking or doing *tai chi,* I feel sluggish and I lose joy. Walking clears my mind, *tai chi* calms my Soul, *yoga* releases my power and dancing frees my Spirit. I return to my natural state of being. I am positive and optimistic. I am a better wife, friend, daughter, teacher and television host; when I am living in balance with movement. Find what your body loves . . . and Move! Move! Move the Body! Now we are ready to *Create Your Space!*

♡ Chapter 6 ♡

Create Your Space

When I was living on the boardwalk of Newport Beach and spiritually growing by leaps and bounds, I decorated my new apartment in purple. Everything in the apartment was a shade of purple. I chose dishes, sheets, pillows, paper, pens, a wallet. All of my clothing ranged from pale lavender to deep purple. These were the only colors to which I could resonate. I was drawn to all items that were purple. Purple moved my heart. I immersed myself on my Spiritual Journey in the color of purple. I absorbed it from around me, as I absorbed the wisdom of the ages from my books. Purple was my passion! I didn't know why. It had just become true to my nature to be in the essence of this vibrant color. My behavior was explained later, when I learned the power of color.

VIBRATIONAL THERAPIES

We taped a series on healing that included vibrational therapies: color, aromatherapy and sound. Here are three fascinating techniques.

Color Therapy

Black has no vibrational energy and is the color of despair. When we have suffered trauma or loss, we may feel and reflect black. Helen Baker, RN, Ph.D. has found that color therapy cannot only move us through the grief process, it can energize or calm us. Succinctly stated; red heightens our physical energy, orange moves us to create, yellow gives us mental energy, green balances us and calms our nerves, blue enhances our communication skills, indigo and purple are spiritually enhancing and white is all of the above. White allows us to be a rainbow of colors, our natural state of bliss. We are in balance when we vibrate with all the colors of the spectrum. Scientific studies have concluded we can diagnose and heal with color. Choose the color to create the result you desire. If you are tired, go to red. If you want to heal or are out of balance, use green. If you want to express yourself, choose blue.

Aromatherapy

Aromatherapy is as old as man. The essential oils were the first medicines. The effects are instantaneous and profound. It is scientifically proven that the olfactory system (smell) has a direct nose/brain link. Split-second effects bring immediate results. Using the essential oils even bolsters the immune system. In liquid form the oils are absorbed through the skin, our largest organ. Sandalwood is one of my favorites, too. I associate it with the Muktananda and my Siddha Yoga experiences. I first smelled the fragrance at a chanting/meditation session in Costa Mesa, California. Sandalwood oil or incense immediately takes me back to that moment and I am able to move into a meditative state more easily. Candace Welsh, the Oil Lady, recommends lavender to balance, peppermint to energize, orange to calm, tea tree oil as an antiviral, antifungal, anti-bacterial medicine and eucalyptus for any breathing disorder. Candace suggested I carry a lavender mist, when I travel by plane. I mist myself and my unsuspecting husband occasionally throughout the flight. There are at least two benefits from the lavender mist. Many people become ill after an airplane trip. The re-circulating air can be disease laden. For years the Europeans have used lavender in their hospitals to clear the air borne bacteria and viruses. The second benefit from misting with this essential oil is the balancing of the central nervous system, as well as the balancing of the rhythms of the body. I have begun to carry orange and peppermint oils with me at all times. I know at a moment's notice I can calm or energize as needed. What a simple technique this is to use.

Music Meditation

One of the most profound physical and spiritual experiences I have ever had, is through music meditation. Joseph Spano, M.D., has employed sound and vibration and music to create a space for people to heal themselves at the Unity Church of Naples, Florida. He has heard miraculous stories over the past 20 years. Cancer in remission, insights gained, problems solved-- participants gave credit to the music meditations. My first personal experience occurred several years ago, when a friend invited me to participate with Dr. Spano's group. Several of us went together and sat in a circle on the floor with pillows under us. He had chosen that evening to play a variety of music, including New Age, classical and rock. Speakers vibrated the floor and our bodies. The physical response led me to believe I was alone. It seemed as if my companions on either side of me had left, gone somewhere. I was alone and felt incredibly at peace. When the meditation ended, I explained my reactions to my friend. She smiled knowingly and suggested that I may have been the one who had left. She said I was describing an *out of body experience*. How fun!

Steven Halpern

Musician and composer Steven Halpern has been a pioneer in the field of healing with music as a vibrational therapy. His music is created with an awareness of its therapeutic effects. When he performs, he feels there are angels with him. Members of his audience often report seeing a band of angels around him. His book, *Tuning the Human Instrument,* has become a textbook on the subject. In a recent interview in Orlando, Florida, Steven suggests we choose the perfect music to enhance our creativity, calm the emotions or open to our spiritual development. Across the top of his stationery are these words in quotations: "Relaxing the body, opening the heart and soothing the soul." What a wonderful effect his music has!

Erik Berglund

Erik Berglund, the internationally renowned musician and harpist, plays angelic music to move the Soul and heal the body. Once a year I invite Erik on our show, when he travels from Mt. Shasta to other parts of the world. Erik first became aware of the healing power of his music when people at a concert in Brazil began to claim physical phenomena--diseases disappeared, health improved. Erik knew his music was enjoyed by his audiences, but he was unaware of the apparent healing *side effects*. Erik has become so popular for his work from Brazil to Germany that he, like Steven Halpern, does workshops on the power of music in mending the body and Spirit.

Words of Wisdom:

"Music soothes the savage beast."

Feng Shui Your Space

Feng shui has been mentioned in a previous chapter. It is defined as the ancient Chinese art of placement for harmony and peace and abundance.

Katrine Karley, a consultant on the topic of spirituality in business, redecorated our television stage and set for "Living in Balance" employing the principles of *feng shui*. She brought a huge jade fish for prosperity, a bright red eight-sided *bagua* for power, crystals and mirrors to change energies, a rabbit's foot fern for abundance. The vibrational shift was profound.

One of my friends has chosen to dedicate her professional life to this practice. She used the principles of *feng shui* and then successfully sold her home for more than the asking price. After a recent speech before the local civic club, she was asked if she could *feng shui* the county jail. They are writing a grant proposal with that purpose in mind. Won't it be fascinating to measure the results of that one?!

Jami Lin

Jami Lin is one of our *Friends* who has shared her wisdom and her Light in our second book. She has created books and videos on the subject of *feng shui*. Jami begins her thoughts for us with these words,

"*Earthbound in this incarnation, it is our birthright to be wonderfully alive, celebrating all earthly delights. Living in balance with Feng Shui is about personal evolution as we create your lives as the Master intended. The magic humans that we are all capable of being, are balanced between body, mind, and spiritual attributes. It is about our purposeful intentions to create better and better lives which is easily done with Feng Shui. It is fun, too!"*

Personally, I employ the principles of *feng shui* in my home and workplace. It is a natural process you may have already done without conscious thought. I recently set aside a room for my tapes from all of my television shows. It now houses every show we have done in a temperature controlled environment. *It just happens to be in the wealth area of the building.* What that means to a *feng shui* consultant is this-- if you were to superimpose the *bagua* over the building, that room would hold my treasures. I do think of my programs as my treasures. Therefore, it was perfect for me to have chosen that space. Another one of my *feng shui* consultant/friends suggested I add little red velvet bows on each shelf with the tapes for greater power. I had already done that! I know a wee bit about the principles of *feng shui*. And, I am a believer. This is so simple and powerful a technique that I think you'll love it and want to use it.

Technique/Process:

"Clear the Clutter"

The first and most simple step in bringing harmony and balance into your environment is to *clear the clutter*. Get rid of all that is not necessary and blocks your path literally and figuratively. Using the old principle of clearing the clutter in your space, clears the clutter in your mind. Whether you clean a closet or organize a drawer, it always works!

The People Principle--Relationships

My whole life has been about relationships. Yours has, too, even if you are not consciously aware of it. Each of us has been aided by or damaged through relationships. They will either support you or block you. The topic is so important, and we can't leave it out. We could include it in every chapter. And, it needs a book of its own. Here are some relationship guidelines:

Love people who support you for your highest and your best.

Invite people into your life who will assist you

on your Spiritual Journey.

Choose positive, optimistic associates.

Spend time with people who encourage your aspirations.

Let go of old friendships that no longer serve you well.

Be the kind of friend you want to have.

Limit contact with family members who are negative.

Re-evaluate the clubs and organizations to which you belong.

Discern people of like mind with whom you may wish to interact.

Find interesting people with new ideas that intrigue you.

Embrace people that stimulate your mind.

Select teachers you want to be like, "when you grow up."

Let your body be a vibrational meter of the energy of the people you encounter. Choose good vibrations!

Affirmation:

I am powerful and capable. I create beauty and love in my life!

Barbara Marx Hubbard

I interviewed futurist and visionary Barbara Marx Hubbard. I asked her about relationships. She defined the modern, spiritual couple. They are in a co-creative relationship. Each person will support the other person's best. They will create the space for the other person to grow. Barbara shared these principles in her book, *The Revelation: A Message of Hope for the New Millennium.* I feel my husband and I fit Barbara's description. Perhaps, the greatest compliment I have ever received was from my father-in-law, Charles Hill. He said I brought out the best in his son. That warmed my heart.

The Universal Laws and Prosperity

Through my reading her books, Catherine Ponder became one of my first teachers of the Universal Laws. I recently had the honor of meeting her at an International New Thought Alliance conference. She was very gracious and looked lovely. I noticed she was being driven in a Rolls Royce limousine. One of her Universal Laws states that, *"Nature abhors a vacuum"* and will fill it. That same principle can be applied to all areas of our lives. You must get rid of the old <u>one</u> that is not perfect to create the space for the Universe to send in the perfect <u>new</u> <u>one!</u> That applies to all areas of our lives--people, jobs, houses, Rolls Royces, etc.

I believe you need to create your physical space. Design as much beauty and harmony and peace as you possibly can in your environment. Use flowers, color, scents and sound. Pay attention to relationships. You have the power and the responsibility to yourself and your personal growth. Now you are ready to find your teachers and pursue the wisdom. We've healed our minds and our bodies. Let's move onto the fun part--freeing the Spirit. Let's *Find Our Teachers* and pursue the wisdom.

Section III "Spirit"

♡ Chapter 7 ♡

Find Your Teachers

On a quiet Saturday afternoon in November of 1983, the pursuit of wisdom took me to a metaphysical bookstore in Costa Mesa, California. This was a new adventure. Although I had been apprehensive, I found the atmosphere was comfortable. A young salesgirl was wearing a long cotton dress and was serving herbal tea. A man was sitting in a big, stuffed chair in the corner. I browsed through the books and found the one that had been recommended to me. The previous week a group of us had driven into Los Angeles to hear Brugh Joy, author of *Joy's Way: A Map for the Transformational Journey*. In his book he had mentioned a spiritual community called Findhorn in northern Scotland. That took us to a gathering in Santa Barbara to meet a young woman from the Findhorn community. She had been one of the designers of *The Transformation Game*. I was so enthralled. I wanted to know more about Findhorn and its educational classes. This little Costa Mesa bookstore had a copy of *Faces of Findhorn*. Just as I was ready to leave, the man in the big overstuffed chair smiled and asked me if I had ever had my astrological chart done. I smiled back and told him no. He introduced himself as Anold, the Astrologer. His service included one free phone call that would answer three brief questions. I took the card with no intention of calling. However, I could not get the idea out of my mind. I was intrigued. And, I had lots of questions that were spinning about in the ethers.

That afternoon started me on a Path that would change my life forever. I have spent the last fifteen years as a student and teacher of spiritual astrology. That part of my journey began with a telephone call to Anold. My three complimentary questions turned into a 45 minute reading. Anold's information and insights were accurate and profound. I was both astounded and convinced. He knew of an extremely important telephone conversation I had the previous day. It was a difficult exchange that had closed a door to the past. Anold spoke of a long trip I would take to another place and another time. He seemed to know my past and my future. I had just been given a gift of a trip to Europe from my sister. My destination would be Findhorn. It was in that beautiful northern Scottish community that I found out what he had meant by *another time.*

Technique/Process:

"Astrology as a Personality Profile"

Please get your chart done and interpreted. There are excellent computer software programs to choose from or find a good, local, *spiritual* astrologer. Mundane astrology is the old-fashioned negative, scary stuff. Before you sit down for a reading, you need to be discerning. If the astrologer does not come highly recommended by a friend, don't go. To be safe, you might want to stick to the computerized version of your life. The software programs I mentioned are accurate and beautifully written with a positive approach to viewing your life's challenges. We have a service with Shakti-Hill House Publishing that will create your chart. We include a natal interpretation and guidelines for the upcoming year. Write us if you would like this information.

Carole Devine

An astrological *Friend* has written a chapter for us in *Sharing the Wisdom and Light*. Carole Devine is a teacher and author on the subject. She wrote of her past experiences in her chapter, Astrology's Quantum Dimension. She explains:

"Around 1969, I discovered Astrology and was shocked to discover that a whole life could be read rather accurately from the day the person was born! I tested it again and again on anyone who would give me a birth date, time and place."

Carole is a wonderful person with high intention. In one of our television interviews on "Living in Balance," she expressed the value of astrology in personal understanding and transformation. Carole has incorporated the philosophy of *A Course in Miracles* with her work on astrological interpretation. That is always a meter that I can use to determine someone's philosophy. You'll enjoy her wisdom in her chapter in our second book.

Eileen Caddy, Findhorn and Past Lives

Cluny College was the place and Experience Week

was the adventure. I saw Eileen Caddy, cofounder of Findhorn, walking down the path at the Caravan Park. She was dressed in a bright, light blue sweater and skirt. She radiated light. Literally, there was a bright, yellow-white light all around her. Later, I realized that I had seen my first aura.

Every day at Findhorn meant another new experience of profound impact. Synchronicity and lessons loomed. One day, as I walked down a country road with a young man from New Zealand, time shifted back to the early 1800's. Our clothes changed, his beard, my hairstyle, everything shifted back and then forward, back and then forward. I had experienced my first *spontaneous past life regression.* We had time-shifted.

During a very quiet moment in the meditation chapel at Cluny College, a voice came to me. My mind had wandered to one of the women in our class, whom I really liked, but could never remember her name. I queried to myself why was I unable to remember Joann's name? It had become embarrassing. The voice quietly spoke inside of my head, "You can't remember her name, because you knew her as Rachel and she was your cousin." I sat frightened, unable to move. When the bell finally jingled to indicate meditation was over, I ran from the room. I blurted out this incredible event to my small group of friends. These wiser companions told me I had heard my own Inner Voice. Gradually the complete story of a past life unfolded. The voice continued to inform me of each person's role. Sometimes I would be awakened in the middle of the night. I was instructed to write down the information. It included most of the people in my class in Experience Week. In addition to Rachel, I had a husband, a son, a mother, a cousin, a father-in-law, etc. I had encountered a group of people who had lived with me in a *past life*. We had come together to heal the issues from that lifetime that had blocked us in this one. I later found out this was not an uncommon occurrence at Findhorn. Just the right people join together in each week's classes for the lessons they need to learn. If by chance the wrong people have gathered, they will not remain. Two people who had started out with our group left. One's wife came and took him home. Another was isolated from us, because he was deathly ill with a life threatening virus that he had caught in transit. We might assume those two did not share our former life together.

I've been drawn back to Scotland and Findhorn since that visit. I read and reread Eileen Caddy's books, *Footprints on the Path* and *God Spoke to Me*. Her philosophy, Experience Week and those events would forever change my perception of this world!

There have been many more journeys in time through these past years. I wouldn't even try to convince you of the truth in past lives. Personally, I have found veracity in each occurrence and it has served me well.

Understanding Past Lives

I interviewed Edward Klein, M.D. of Tampa, Florida. He has written an excellent book on the subject, *Healing Possibilities of Past Lives*. Through his research with his patients, he has documented hundreds of cases of regressions to another time and place. It gives him another tool for healing.

Janet Cunningham, Ph.D., author of *A Tribe Returned*, has received fascinating information on past lives. Janet is one of our *Friends* with a chapter in the second book. She wrote:

" *Past lives are not in the past--they are here, NOW; we carry them in our energy field, or mind field. The value of a past life regression is not to remember who we were, but to more fully grasp who we **are**--today. We are a product of everything that has come before . . . from birth and before birth. It is all reflected in our personality and being through loves, hopes, fears, likes and dislikes, and struggles of life.*"

I would trust both Dr. Klein and Dr. Cunningham to assist me in a past life regression. I *feel* they are well intentioned and they have credentials and years of experience behind them. There is always a gift from the past that can serve us well in this lifetime. It is just wise to choose a hypnotherapist who is well qualified and well intentioned.

Technique/Process:

"A Past Life Regression"

If you have never had a spontaneous past life regression, you can regress yourself or find a good therapist. Trust is important when working with a therapist. Carl Jung, the great Swiss psychiatrist, was very hesitant and cautious about hypnosis. He said you are quite open and vulnerable during the process. He explained that you psychically connect with the other individual. Make sure you are merging with someone of integrity and ability. The therapist must come highly recommend by someone you respect. There are excellent tapes you can purchase and books you can read about doing self-hypnosis for past life work. Although it may not be as effective or profound as working with a counselor, it is easy and fun and safe. Dick Supthen has a monologue for you to create your own tape in his book, *Finding Your Answers Within.*

Affirmation:

Show me the Truth in this!
(Affirm and then wait for the Universe to answer.)

Our teachers are everywhere in our lives. Each person that I interview on my television show is my teacher. I listen and I learn. I read and I question. The Burmese Buddhist monk, the Swami from Sri Lanka, the Tibetan professor, the Sufi master, the Shaman from South America, the chief and high holy man from New Zealand, they are all my teachers--the authors and artists and musicians and ministers and healers. We meet for a short time and they share their Wisdom and we share the Light.

About Eddie and "the Boys"

My husband, Eddie, is a powerful teacher for me in this lifetime. He has taught me love and devotion. He also has a calmness about him that I try to emulate. He is refreshingly playful. I find his unique perspectives on events both interesting and insightful. He has a clarity of perception I trust. He is discerning and very discriminating. I honor our differences and try to learn from them. I appreciate our likenesses and find them reassuring. Eddie is my teacher.

And, so are my Boys. They are three twelve-year-old Siamese cats: Mango, Dax and Leo. The boys teach me patience and gentleness and harmlessness. But, the greatest gift these three precious little beings have taught me is the gift of unconditional love. Oh, if I could only carry that over into all of my human interactions . . . if we ALL could carry that over into our human relationships, the world would be a wondrous place.

Affirmation:

I accept love and support in my life and share it with others.

Words of Wisdom:

"To love for the sake of being loved is human, But to love for the sake of loving is angelic."

--*Alphonse de Lamartine, Graziella*

More Love and Support

I am so fortunate to be part of a large, loving family. I have three sisters and have been blessed with nieces and nephews, whom I adore. Each one is special to me. What a gift it is to love and be loved by so many. We are thousands of miles apart geographically, but are always close at heart. Next to my husband, my mother is my greatest supporter. My sisters and I have a deep and mutual love and respect for each other. I cherish these relationships and I remember to give thanks for them. I am very lucky and I know it. Thank you, God!

Professionally, I am blessed with staff and crew and volunteers. Cookie, my make-up artist is

Hollywood-trained and has been with me from the beginning. She had aspired to work on the crew of "Touched by An Angel" and figured we were the next closest thing. Christina is a "volunteer" who advises me on a variety of subjects from wardrobe to book covers. She is a highly evolved spiritual being and I trust her judgment and sincerity. Diana and Donna have recently joined us and are willing to do everything. Our talented and professional director, production manager, camera people and editors support our efforts beautifully. You need to have harmony on the set and among the production team. A show like "Living in Balance" could not be created by unevolved, angry people. If our crew and staff were ego-oriented and power-driven, it would negatively affect the program. Eddie, my husband, is always in the control room or on location with us. I laugh and say, "It is a very good idea to have someone who loves you in the control room."

Technique/Process:

"Honor Your Teachers"

List your most powerful teachers. Honor them for the lessons they have taught you. Remember the lessons could have come from love and could have been gentle. Some lessons might have been tough and seemed cruel. Our most profound lessons may come from the pain we suffer in the process. Perhaps some of your teachers have been beautiful and loving. Others may have been harsh and difficult. You learned from each. Thank them all.

Affirmation:

There is a gift in this experience. All is well.

Words of Wisdom:

"When the student is ready, the teacher appears."

James Twyman, Peace Troubadour

James Twyman, the peace troubadour, wrote about the Masters he met in *Emissary of Light*. He traveled to far away Bosnia, into the hills. His teachers shared with him their wisdom and their

Light. He is now spreading the word. Jimmy and I talked and he sang for us. His fabulous message of peace and hope comes through his music and meditations. He was directed to create a peace song for each of the twelve major religions of the world. He has invited our audience to participate in the festivals of synchronicity for peace. The new millennium is at hand.

It is appropriate for *you* to find your teachers. Take a class. Go to church. Study the books. Be open to life's lessons. Recognize the gift in the lesson. Question and ask. Does it ring true? Does it resonate? Can you own it as your philosophy and truth? Your teachers are your companions and guides on the Path. They might awaken, educate or entertain you. They will help you take the steps to enlightenment. Remember, when the student is ready, the teacher appears. Now you are ready to *Meet the Masters*.

♡ Chapter 8 ♡

Meet the Masters

As you evolve spiritually, you will become your own best counselor. Your intuitive abilities will become so precise that you will not choose to go outside yourself for advice. As you open to the flow of the Universe, you will *know* what to do. If you have not reached that point, you will. It is one of the rewards on the Path. The power does not come until you are ready for it. Psychic ability is natural and it will become a part of you, as you mature on the Journey. In the meantime, as you are waiting to trust yourself and your own intuitive abilities, I do not recommend that you go from one psychic to another in search of answers or guidance. Never, never return to a psychic who has made you either fearful or sad. There are thousands of Old Souls out there with a desire to help you with your spiritual evolution. Discerning the great ones may be a difficult task. Trust your instinct and get referrals.

Mediums

Ron Warmoth of Los Angeles, Rev. Ruth Ann McGrath of Cape Coral, Florida, and John C. White of Lilydale, New York, are three mediums I have recently re-interviewed. Each had correctly predicted in the previous programs that my television show would be picked up nationally. Each indicated we would have an international audience. I had not asked them for the information. Each had volunteered it. Even their timing had been *right on!* I know some people are better at predictions than others. I just don't recommend you give your power away to a person of questionable veracity or integrity.

Intuition

Lynn Robinson of Massachusetts and Scottish born Laura Anne Walker are intuitives, who teach techniques in developing your own psychic or intuitive abilities. They can counsel you and share with you the information you need to take that next step toward awakening your own innate abilities. In our television interview Lynn said, "Training people how to use their intuition, that is my passion in life. I love doing that. To me it is such a practical skill to have. I really do think we all have it. Some of us have developed it more than others . . . not unlike someone being born with an athletic ability or a musical ability."

During our interview Laura Anne Walker shared her favorite techniques for Intuitive Development. Practice meditating or spending quiet time reflecting, while you are listening for that Inner Voice to become louder. Ask the question and then listen for the answer. I love her definition of intuition. She defines it in this way:

"Intuition is the link between our soul and our higher, or Divine, self. When we develop and incorporate it into our daily lives, we function effortlessly and live in harmony and balance."

Tools of Divination

On those rare and awful occasions when I have become terribly upset over an issue, I want to get the lesson in it and move forward. When I am unable to move past it or resolve it, I want to understand the issue and move on! When I am in a state of confusion, I want clarity. When I am dumbfounded,

I want to know why! It is at those times I turn to a "tool of Divination." My preference is the *I Ching*. The *I Ching* translates to the Chinese Book of Changes. It is thousands of years old and carries the wisdom of the ages. I consult four different versions of the book for interpretation of the message. Carl Jung has been quoted in saying that had he found it sooner, he could have spent thirty years of his life studying the *I Ching*. It has served me well over the years and has an uncanny knack of always addressing the issue at hand.

Technique/Process:

"Consulting the Oracle of the *I Ching*"

Borrow a book on the *I Ching* from the library or invest in one. I approach my inquiry with great reverence, as if I were actually in the presence of the Chinese oracle. Ask a serious and important question. Write the question in precise and clear terms. Read the instructions for casting the coins or sticks. Follow the directions and go through the process. Read the interpretation and see if you connect to the energy of the *I Ching* and its oracle. You will find it fascinatingly accurate, as Carl Jung and I have, or you may think it ridiculous. If it works for you, you have met one of your mystics and you have connected with an oracle who can serve you well in times of confusion and doubt.

The Runes

Richard Blum wrote *The Book of Runes*. I acquired a set of the stones with the book when living on the beach in California. I realized Blum and I were philosophically attuned, when I noted his bibliography included *A Course in Miracles* and some of Jung's works. I resonated to his spiritual interpretation of the ancient stones of the Vikings and Norse mythology. Even when the stones come up in reverse, he is not negative in his message. The reader is simply facing a challenge that will have a positive end result. Blum gave the Runes wonderful names like Breakthrough and Growth. I consult the Runes when I have a small dilemma and I can't quite get the message I need from the Universe. I pull one Rune. This is referred to as Odin's Rune. I ask, "What is the lesson in this issue and what do I need to know to move through it?" If the issue is a little more complex, I pull three runes: situation, action required and the end result. I ask, "What is the best that can be accomplished in this situation." I could relate phenomenal information that has come to me and my family and friends through the Runes. That would take another book.

Mikki and Alex--A Love Story

I kept the Runes at our cafe on Fort Myers Beach. I would allow my close associates to consult the Runes, if needed. One of my friends was extremely reluctant to get involved in relationship. She had met a man at one of our Festivals of Synchronicity on the beach. They had been meeting for coffee and he seemed interested in her on a personal level. Enjoying her power and independence, she was hesitant to allow him into her life. However, every time she pulled a Rune, the great **X** would come into her hand indicating *Partnership.* This happened every time. She became upset with the Runes. I simply explained the Universe supported her working on relationship again. This time it could be from a spiritual perspective and it could be positive. What she really needed to do with the Runes was pull another one to teach her the *lesson* in relationship she needed to learn. She listened. Mikki and Alex married. They are together, sharing happily in a loving, supportive partnership. They have a co-creative relationship. The Runes served her well.

Technique/Process:

"Animal Medicine"

Ted Andrews is a prolific author and lover of nature. His book *Animal Speak* is an absolutely fabulous reference book for divining an answer from your environment. In our interview for "Living in Balance," Ted shared his wisdom and his Light through his publications. He explained how he looks for a totem animal in each endeavor, activity, workshop, class, etc. to gain an insight into the lesson. I refer to *Animal Speak* to get direction or see what energies are working in an incident or circumstance. The native American philosophy includes a quality or characteristic of each animal. Ted has taken that to a fuller meaning in his book. You have a greater understanding and gain insights, when you pay attention to the world around you. The messages are there. There is another tool of divination, the Animal Medicine Cards that has served me well. Each day I have been writing this book, I have journaled the animals that have come into my life--turtle, chickadee, a bluebird, an ant, etc. Each chapter has had an animal totem. It is fun!

Tara Singh

Tara Singh sent me a lovely note after our interview regarding *A Course in Miracles*. Our entire crew had been caught in a *holy instant* that lasted throughout the afternoon. Tara wrote:

*"The fact is that **nothing happens** by **chance** and the harmony between us all was the Given. Wherever there is stillness, there is a warmth that we all share. I am glad that we appreciate the moments together."*

I knew our time together was very special. He smiled and wisely told his story with energy and excitement. I refer to Tara Singh as a *high holy man*. He has been a prolific author and lecturer on the subject of the Course. Being in his presence was a gift to all of us that day. He spoke of the Course in such loving terms. He called it the one great scripture written in this time and in this place. I, too, have been a student/teacher of this course for many years. It is profound and requires a commitment of time and Spirit.

The Masters and Angels

I recently reread *At the Feet of the Masters* and *The Life and Teachings of the Masters from the Far East*. The lessons are profound. These and other books are such wonderful reminders of the Universal Laws and Truths. I love White Eagle's works. You can open to any page and read exactly what you need to know. Paramahansa Yogananda's *The Divine Romance* is just such a collection of writings. Begin at any point and you will receive the message needed. All of John Randolph Price's books share the basic truths. That is how the Masters' writings serve us so well.

Look to the Star

When I was ten years old, I met my Master teacher. I didn't know it at the time. But it is an event that is perfectly clear in my mind today. I was at a Lutheran church camp in southern Ohio, Camp Mowana. It was my first time away from home and I was in deep and dreadful despair. I was looking up at a dark sky full of stars and I was crying hard. Through the tears one of the stars turned into Jesus. His outstretched arms seemed to reach to me and I was comforted. I never spoke of it to anyone. It wasn't necessary. My week of crafts and activities finished on a happy note.

Words of Wisdom:

Look to the Star

"When you are in the shadow ... remember to look up, to visualize the blazing Star above you ... feel its strength, its steadiness, its radiance pouring into your heart."

--White Eagle, The Quiet Mind

Meeting my Master Teacher

Years later, but early on in my study of metaphysics and spiritual development, I participated in a process called "Meeting Your Master Teacher." I had my second encounter with Jesus. How presumptuous of me, I thought. How incredibly pompous to think the Son of God would come to me in this meditation. I was embarrassed to tell anyone about our meeting. Farther down the Path I was counseled by those wiser than I. They explained that Jesus serves many as Master Teacher. He is ready when we call. There have been a few times that I have needed his protection. He has always been there for me. I seldom ask, however. It still seems again to be a bit presumptuous of me. It is at those times, when I do choose to call upon him; I want to be very clear on what I seek.

Canceling a Meeting with my Guides

In the midst of my search for the Truth, I kept reading about my Guides. Apparently, they were there like the Masters and Angels to assist me along my Path. Everyone else on their Spiritual Journey seemed to be using their Guides to great benefit. I decided one night that it was time to meet them. I was lying in bed on a hot summer night in Laguna Hills, California, at a sister's home. I went into a deep meditation. My eyes were closed and my intention was serious and reverent. I invited my Guides to come and be with me, to make themselves known to me. At that precise moment the bed began to shake eerily and the room seemed to roll. I quickly and simply said, "Never mind!" The movement stopped. I realized I wasn't truly ready to encounter the Divine Beings in charge of my

Spiritual growth after all. The next morning I found out that southern California had suffered another mild earthquake. I still ponder the experience.

Words of Wisdom:

"For every soul, there is a guardian watching it."

--*The Koran*

Back to Angels

Now, with the angels, I ask for guidance and assistance all the time. There is an angel in charge of everything. There is an angel of the roses. An angel oversees my country home. There is an angel of the pond. There is an angel of my television show. In the studio, on any set or anywhere we are on location, we invoke the Divine at the beginning of every program. I first learned to incorporate this process at Findhorn. They referred to it as attuning to the space. We hold hands in a circle and our prayer for the show begins:

"Taking just a few deep breaths, bring your full attention to the here and now.

As we do, we bring down the Divine white Light, that surrounds us and protects

So that all that we do is for the highest and the best.

All that we share is our love, our peace and our Light.

As always, our purpose is to heal.

We do invite the Angel of 'Living in Balance on Shakti-Hill' to be with us today.

Namaste *and welcome."*

An angel joins me on every show. We have one over my shoulder and others here and there on the set. I have an angel of my car in my car. I give them to people I love, who need them as a reminder. Angels are assigned to us and they oversee the events in our lives. When I sat down at the computer to begin this book, I chose an angel to be with me for the entire project. She has served me well, too. Patricia Sistrunk is an angel artist. She sees and talks to angels. She wrote and illustrated a book entitled " . . . *and the angel said* . . . " She sent me a list of thoughts the angels had shared with her. One is *"Angels are part of humankind's Reality, and they will be more visible, much more frequently, from now on."*

(By the way, look up in an angel's presence. Patricia says they are quite tall. And, she did mention that they prefer to visit with you in the early morning hours.)

Nick Bunick and *The Messengers*

Nick Bunick of *The Messengers* told our audience during an interview for "Living in Balance," that the angels are bringing through a message to us for the new millennium. The three guidelines they ask us to follow are: speak the Truth, share Universal Love and Universal Compassion. Nick wrote about the "4-4-4" phenomenon. Some have questioned the message. I resonated to his words, because I had been experiencing the "4-4-4" phenomenon for years. I use the 4's as Divine feedback, confirmation from the Universe that what I am doing is right on! In numerology four is my destiny number. I believed that the triple fours indicated it was my destiny. They would appear when I had a question or was confused. I would notice them on license plates, on addresses, in telephone numbers, etc. I queried Nick about my history with the 4-4-4 and he said that I was correct to use it as Divine feedback. To him it represents the power of God. The angels speak to us in many ways.

A Very Personal Angel Story

My nephew Michael was lying gravely ill in a hospital in California. I was in Florida and feeling very concerned for him. His mother called me and said Michael's condition was grave and he needed our prayers. Having been trained and initiated as a Reiki Master, I learned a process called "absentee healing." In Level Two Reiki you are taught that you can send energy across thousands of miles in an instant. There is a process and a symbolical procedure that you execute. Sitting quietly, I methodically went through the healing meditation. However, at the end I adapted the Reiki process to fit into my own personal philosophy that included angels. I envisioned Michael surrounded in a white light and I asked an angel to enfold him. I held that image in my mind and sat very quietly in prayer. I am so choked with emotion that I can barely type this. It is very personal to impart to you what happened next. I pondered whether it was too private. I feel you may benefit from our experience. So, I continue the story. Within minutes my sister called me and she was crying. She didn't know what I had been doing. She wanted to share with me a beautiful happening. Although Michael was blind, he had *seen* an angel standing in the corner of his hospital room. The angel was shining like pure white crystal, as she came to him and held him. Michael survived that crisis.

Affirmation:

I am surrounded with the love of angels.

Technique/Process:

"White Lighting"

I could not write this book without included the *White Lighting* technique. It is a powerful tool to use every day of your life. To "white light"someone or something is to put a protective energy field around the subject. It has been described as a bell jar of protection dropped around a person. It can be visualized as a soft cloud encircling your home, your husband, your car, your project. It brings a Divine vibration. When someone is especially difficult to deal with or is in great need of assistance, you can invoke the angels to help. I usually say, "Surround them in Love and hold them in the Light."

Mind, body and Spirit bring us into balance. All three come into play. On this Path to Enlightenment we are evolving and growing and learning to be channels of love. The road home is sometimes splashed with tears. We need only remember we have companions who will join us on the journey-- the Masters whom we know and love and the angels who are just waiting at our beck and call. We can ask for Divine guidance or Divine wisdom at each turn and with every step. With the Masters' and the angels' assistance we can fulfill our purpose on the planet. That is why we are here. If you have not found your purpose and how you can *Fulfill Your Dharma,* read on.

♡ Chapter 9 ♡

Fulfill Your Dharma

During our most recent conversation on television with the SwamiYogeshwarananda, I asked and he explained *dharma* to me in this way: "*Your dharma is not just your purpose in life. It is your natural talent and ability.*" For the first time I understood. Clarity came with the idea of a *natural gift*. What is true to your nature? What were you born to share with others? What is your purpose in this lifetime and on this planet? What is your highest aspiration? Define your role in the big picture.

Words of Wisdom:

"Your work is to discover your work and

then with all your heart to give yourself to it."

--*the Buddha*

Joseph Campbell called it *following your bliss*. Being the host of "Living in Balance," is definitely following my bliss. To do this is a blessing from God. Heaven is shining down on me and the angels are my friends. I LOVE what I do. The fascinating part of this concept is that so many people are searching for their purpose. Karen Mc Coy is an excellent author and astrologer that I have interviewed several times. She coauthored *Spiritual Astrology*. The book lists the lunar and solar eclipses that preceded your birth. The lunar eclipse represents what you are here to learn. The astrological sign in which the solar eclipse occurred tells you what you are here to teach. I recall my purpose is *to shine the light upon other people in order that they, too, may fulfill their purpose*. How better could we do that than with the bright lights that shine upon our television guests as they share their wisdom and their Light? Let's interpret this literally. Our lighting people spend a great deal of time making sure the light shines best on our "talent." People in the business will often say, "Lighting is everything!"

That literal translation of my *dharma* is not the

only definition that works for me. I LOVE what I do. Smiling into a camera is as comfortable for me, as sitting and holding one of my cats and sipping a cup of tea. Asking questions of my guests, excites and intrigues me. Searching for their passion and finding the essence of their message, is my quest. Seeking, searching and pursuing their *truth*, drives me. I love what I do! It takes me at least an hour to calm down after a shoot. My adrenalin has been flowing. My power is high! I have been enthralled and engrossed. The time has flown by and I was unaware. My longest day includes a ten-hour shoot. At a recent conference my last thirty-minute interview was with Steven Halpern, the musician and healer. I was as excited and as energetic at the end of my day, as I was with my first guest nine hours earlier. One day on location in Sedona, Arizona, I interviewed seventeen guests. That is just the way it all worked out. The talent appeared and I wanted to hear each story. I kept my energy high . . . I had the power to carry on!

The Audience Response

Recently, a Florida woman who regularly watches our program, called and gave me a huge compliment. She said I was "delightful and my childlike enthusiasm shown over the televison screen." She absolutely made my day. Bless her for sharing that thought. When you love it, it shows!

A viewer from New York wrote,

"Your programs . . . are a delight. You probably don't share in every belief expressed by every guest on your show, but you always treat everyone graciously, with charm and intelligence. I particularly like the slack you give your guests and then the way you tighten the reins and get them to summarize more precisely what they've been saying. Or sometimes you do the summing up yourself, and you do it masterfully."

No kinder words have ever been written. My audience is so important to me. My honesty, sincerity and integrity *must* come across the air waves. If they do not, the people won't continue to watch and learn. I must be authentic.

And Messages Come by e-mail

E-mail is a great way to receive communication from our viewers. Julie recently sent this message over the Internet:

"I'd like to compliment you on your program. It provides unique information and perspective in an intelligent and tasteful way. Georgia is truly a blessing for those who are 'searching.'"

How could you not love what you do, when people are so kind and appreciative?

Words of Wisdom:

"Work is love made visible."

--Kahlil Gibran

Technique/Process:

"Personal Inventory and History"

I can look back over my life and realize, everything I have ever done has brought me to this point. All the major events and traumas of my life unfolded exactly as they did in order for me to be in this place at this time. My education, my career choices, relationships, moves and pursuits were all factors leading to *the here and now*. An illness was a gift, a dis-ease was an adventure that played out with a positive result. Parcels of real estate I couldn't buy, or one I couldn't sell, were all factors. I had the perfect father and mother to send me on my Journey. All has been in Divine order. People fulfilling their *dharma* tell me they have come to this same conclusion. Ask yourself in what direction are you heading? What have all the lessons been about? How does your past support your spiritual future? Where does your Path lead?

Affirmation:

All is in Divine order.

Lessons on the Path

There is a flow to the Universe. There is a Path for each of us. As we take the appropriate steps, there is an ease to our Journey. I love it when I am going with the flow. You know it, you experience it and your life is wonderful! Everything falls into place. The *Force* is with you. The abundance is there. The check is in the mail. The offer arrives. The contract is signed. When it is working, you skip quickly and lightly along your Path. You are *following your bliss.*

When we step off the Path, take a "wrong" turn, we will only suffer a delay. Detours are lessons we are choosing to learn. If we do not get back on the Path in this lifetime, reincarnation gives us an opportunity to come back and do it again. We can get it right this time or we can return, until we accomplish our true goal. Choose again.

The Universe supports us when we are going with its flow. If they don't call, don't buy, don't support, don't attend--something is wrong. I repeat, "The Universe whispers and then it shouts." If you don't get the message, the words become stronger and harsher. Persistence is required along with tenacity and industriousness. Don't misunderstand the point. If you have created the best possible product, program or idea and you find that nobody responds-- regroup. Step back and reflect. Ask for Divine guidance. Know that you will be rewarded when you have connected to your higher purpose. That is what is required of you. A defeat is a powerful and positive message to go in another direction. A delay allows you to correct it, make changes and move on. Sometimes the lesson is simply to detach from the result. Do not depend on a defined outcome. Do not impose expectations. Each challenge makes you stronger and more able to cope. Success is the inevitable result of your connecting to your higher purpose and fulfilling your *dharma*. If it did not happen, it simply was not meant to be. Trust destiny!

Words of Wisdom:

"Let there be no feeling of competition within you. When you realize that each of you has your specific part to play in the whole, all that spirit of competition will disappear, and you will be able to relax and be yourself."

--*Eileen Caddy*, Footprints on the Path

The First Goal of Ayurveda

Rajan Sareen, M.D. has given us permission to reprint an excerpt from his publication *Blissful Health, Through Reduction of Stress.* He explained the Ayurvedic philosophy to us during an interview on "Living in Balance." Ayurveda is an ancient system of healing from India in which the mind and body can function only if there is a reflection of the Divine Spirit. According to Dr. Sareen and Ayurveda, there are four goals of life. The most important of these is Essence of Duty or *dharma*. Your duty is threefold. Manifest your Divine nature. Serve humanity. Express your unique talent. Not to do so will create stress. Dr. Sareen shares more wisdom in our second book *Sharing the Wisdom and Light*.

Words of Wisdom:

"Use me, O God, as Thou seest I may better serve Thee: in my waking moments, in my walls and my dealings with my fellow man, be Thou the guide."

--Edgar Cayce, Reading 442-3

Expressing Your Unique Gift

In our interviews many of our guests have expressed this same idea in their own personal terminologies. The message is the same. They connect with the sublime. Author and lecturer, Mark Wenner, referred to being *in the zone*. Athletes feel it and we can watch them perform incredible feats, when they are *in the zone*. Al Oerter said he knew he was *home,* when he picked up the discus that earned him four Olympic gold medals. Dean Martens, the stockbroker-turned herbalist, could not abandon his pursuit of the healthy lifestyle. It became his *passion.* When angel artist, Ann Rothan, is inspired, she is *compelled* to paint. Candace Welsh, an aromatherapist, said it beautifully, "You find your river and you go with your flow. I was *born* to do this." That is fulfilling your *dharma.*

They Are Serving Us

Marianne Williamson is awakening our political consciousness. Eve Haverfield is saving the sea turtles. Sue Blair has created a community for learning. Rama Vernon is resolving personal and global conflicts. Marci Shimoff is writing books with lessons in love and life. Dr. Martin Price is fighting world hunger at ECHO. Robin Miller and Iasos are writing songs. Don Alberto is connecting the condor and the eagle. Dan Millstein is working in prisons. Mandy Evans is offering happiness options. Pat Rodegast is channeling the ancient wisdom through Emmanuel. Rosemary Ellen Guilley is telling of angels. Margaret Jackson and Michael Irvine are capturing beauty for us with photography. Delmary and Katra Marie Peck portray beauty with paint. Ernestine Cline draws your teachers and guides. The beautiful Lani Yamasaki represents her Hawaiian people and their culture. These are all loving Spirits I have interviewed. There are hundreds more who are serving us well.

Ruth Montgomery and Mary Lou Keller

I have had the honor of sharing Ruth Montgomery with our audience. She is called the *Herald of The New Age*. Thirty years ago Ruth was a pioneer on the subject of metaphysics and spirituality in the United States. It was brave of her to write of such subjects, when she risked a successful Washington, D.C., journalism career. Ruth is a very special woman. Her books were among the first metaphysic to be written in America and she fascinated the world with her topics: *Here and Hereafter, Aliens Among Us, Companions Along the Way*. We are enriched because of her indomitable Spirit. She chose to write. It was her *dharma*.

Mary Lou Keller has been credited as the founder of the metaphysical and spiritual community of Sedona, Arizona. Many have bestowed upon her the title of "The Gatekeeper." She doesn't relish the label, but allows others to think what they may.

Mary Lou has recently written a book on her life and the lives of other Sedonans. She will be in our second book *Sharing the Wisdom and Light*. Here is an excerpt from her Introduction:

"Long ago, when only Native Americans knew this spectacular high desert country, they considered this valley of red rock spires, energy vortexes and mysterious hidden canyons to be sacred ground. It seems this mystique still lingers over Sedona, for among the approximately 4,000,000 tourists who visit here during a single year, many will return on a spiritual vision quest. Numerous people who live here will tell you that Sedona has totally enchanted and bewitched them and they cannot stay away."

Had Mary Lou Keller not fulfilled her *dharma* and ventured to Sedona and created the spiritual space for others to share, millions would have been affected. She walked her path and pioneered a place for healing and growth. Bless her for her courage. At the age of 84 she can look back with pride and look forward to her fascinating Journey. Both she and Ruth followed their bliss, against all odds and all negative forces. They walked their Paths.

Technique/Process:

"Following Your Bliss"

First ask yourself these questions?

What would you do, even if they didn't pay you?

What gifts, talents and natural abilities do you have?

What are you told that you do "so well?"

What are your hobbies?

What do you do in your free time?

What is your dream, your vision?

When are you the happiest?

What do you do with ease?

Second, ask the big question: **"Do these gifts, talents, abilities, hobbies, activities *serve others*?"**

That is the other part of the *dharma* picture. Find it and share it. The Universe will support you in your endeavor, if you are serving others. It will be your highest and your best. You will be *following your bliss . . . fulfilling your dharma!*

Affirmations:

I am going with the flow of the Universe. I follow my bliss.

Living in Balance in Mind, Body and Spirit, you can fulfill your purpose and follow your bliss. That is why you are on this planet in this lifetime. That is why you were born to--share your wisdom and *Share your Light.*

Blessings,

G. Shakti-Hill

About the Author

Georgia Shakti-Hill is a television talk show host and motivational speaker. Her programs air over the Wisdom Channel and PBS. She has earned a Master's degree with an emphasis on psychology and sociology. Her background is education and her business experience adds a dimension of practicality that comes across. She has studied the world religions and traveled the globe. Her personal training in stress management, creative visualization, astrology, herbology, Reiki, yoga, tai chi, nutrition and the ancient wisdoms qualifies her as an excellent interviewer and source of information. Over the past seven years she has hosted "Star Talk" and "Mind, Body, Spirit" and is currently the host of "Living in Balance on Shakti-Hill." Her special talent is in shining the light on her guests and bringing out their best information to share with her audience. She knows how to ask questions and get the answers that mainstream America can comprehend. Her greatest assets are her credibility and her open, humorous approach to her topics. Shakti-Hill is a much sought after keynote speaker. Her message is positive and inspirational. With this book she can assist you on your journey back to bliss, peace, health and abundance.

We hope you enjoyed this Shakti-Hill House book. If you would like to receive a list of videos featuring Georgia and her guests or an audio cassette of this book, please contact:

Shakti-Hill House Publishing
P.O. Box 2715
Fort Myers Beach, FL 33932-2715

941-463-8088

Please visit the Shakti-Hill web site at:
www.shakti-hill.com